THE ROYAL TENENBAUMS

THE ROYAL TENENBAUMS

Wes Anderson

&

Owen Wilson

ff

Faber and Faber, Inc.

An affiliate of Farrar, Straus and Giroux

New York

First published in 2001
by Faber and Faber Limited
3 Queen Square London WCIN 3AU
Published in the United States by Faber and Faber, Inc.
an affiliate of Farrar, Straus and Giroux LLC, New York

Wes Anderson and Owen Wilson are hereby
identified as authors of this work in accordance with
Section 77 of the Copyright, Designs and Patents Act 1988

A CIP record for this book
is available from the British Library

ISBN 0-571-21545-9

Typeset by Country Setting, Kingsdown, Kent CT14 8ES
Originally printed in England by Mackays of Chatham plc, Chatham, Kent
First U.S. printing, 2002

www.fsgbooks.com

4 6 8 10 9 7 5 3

CONTENTS

INTRODUCTION

Although I asked Orson Welles ten different ways why he put his camera in a certain unusual place for one of his movies, I nearly always received the same basic answer: he simply thought the scene looked better from there. Occasionally, he apologised for being less than illuminating. When I asked why he had shown a moment from such an 'odd angle', he said that to him it 'wasn't odd'. Exasperated after a series of this sort of questions, Welles finally told me that he was actually just like the man in the joke who goes to his doctor and says, 'I don't know what's the matter with me, Doc, but I just don't feel right.' So the doctor says, 'All right – well, tell me everything you do from the moment you wake up till you go to sleep.' The guy says, 'OK – well, I wake up, then I vomit, then I brush my . . . ' 'Wait a second,' the doctor says, 'you mean right after you wake up every morning you vomit?' The man says, 'Yeah, doesn't everybody?' Orson smiled. 'That's me and my supposedly strange way of seeing things. To me it all seems quite normal.'

To Wes Anderson, as well, his own vision seems quite normal, yet it is as uniquely (and recognisably) his as Welles', and equally without self-conscious pretensions. Also like Welles, Wes is one of those rare picture-makers who can see the whole movie in his head long before he shoots. This gift gives him during filming, of course – since he's already seen it in his mind's eye – a very strong sense of what exactly he wants. The script of *The Royal Tenenbaums* – written by Wes and his usual writing partner Owen Wilson (who also gives a spirited, complicated performance in a key role) – is a perfect blueprint for the finished film. The draft I read just before they started shooting is essentially the movie Wes made, and I thought the script was brilliant. The picture is superb. The amazing cast of star actors are each perfectly chosen for their roles, not surprising because Wes and Owen wrote pretty much all the roles with the same players in mind. Many people have a dream cast they write for but know they'll never get; Wes just wouldn't take no for an answer, and finally got them all. His laid-back attitude seemed to be (this was unspoken) that he'd already seen them in the film and knew they were going to be great, so why would they *not* do it?

Apart from his gifts of visualisation, Anderson's determination to get his own way – his relentless tenacity – marks him conclusively as a born picture-maker. This is not a question of ego, either, but rather an essential character trait in a field where three hundred different opinions and five hundred alternative possibilities have to be dealt with quickly and efficiently. All these muscular abilities are in direct contrast to the way Anderson looks or conducts himself personally. He is rail-thin, bookish, somewhat tweedy, polite, soft-spoken, shy – a terribly nice, intelligent, pleasant-looking, quick-witted, and insatiably curious young Texan from Houston. Wilson, on the other hand, who was first seen in *Bottle Rocket* (1996) – the first film Anderson and Wilson wrote and Anderson directed – has very quickly become recognised as a star performer of quirky dramatic and comic genius.

The Royal Tenenbaums grew directly out of Anderson's desire to make a film in New York City. He had moved here after the release of the wonderful second film Anderson and Wilson wrote, *Rushmore* (1998). I remember Wes telling me at the time that he wanted to do a movie about an eccentric family of New Yorkers living in a large house somewhere in Manhattan. I suggested a couple of plays or movies for him to check out, and he spent a long time alone and with Owen (who acted in a couple of movies in the meantime) – getting familiar with New York and stories of families in this city. The disparate influences on the final work might be apparent to some: J. D. Salinger's Glass family, Kaufman and Hart, Dawn Powell, Orson Welles. But *The Royal Tenenbaums* is very much its own thing, and stands out as an exceptionally gifted, quirky and original director's triumphant third work – his best so far.

There's the same wry wit behind all three Anderson pictures, and each has the same degree of self-confidence. Polly Platt – Anderson's first producer, along with James L. Brooks – told me that on *Bottle Rocket* she could immediately tell he was talented because of the total assurance he had about what he wanted, indeed his insistence on it – all to the good because the movie is a thoroughgoing delight: a charmingly perverse, mordantly funny look at a particular boy-man's world that defines in microcosm an awful lot of the male syndrome.

The film attracted little audience attention but led none the less to Wes and Owen's breakthrough with *Rushmore*, the story of another kind of outsider, a sort of artistic overachieving freak of a teenager in a world of conformity. The idea of the overachiever is taken to even greater and more varied lengths in *The Royal Tenenbaums*, but what ties the three films together is not so much their thematic similarities as their particular style, which lies in the personality of the picturemaker. When I once asked Howard Hawks which directors over the years he had liked best, he replied: 'I liked almost anybody that made you realise who in the devil was making the picture . . . Because the director's the storyteller and should have his own method of telling it.' With a Wes Anderson film, you know who the devil made it, yet his style is as difficult to describe as only the best styles are, because they're subtle.

Perhaps the device of the book and the narrator which Anderson and Wilson adopted for *The Royal Tenenbaums* creates a more easily describable style but that's actually only a technique. It does, however, in some ways help to define the indirect, elliptical, yet often emotionally resonant Anderson touch. I'm especially glad that Wes is so young, because now we all have a great many Wes Anderson pictures to look forward to. He brings a particular quality to his people, a kind of warmth and humanity seen from a wickedly humorous perspective that is at the same time compassionate. Because his movies are exceedingly likeable, with a kind of knowing innocence, it could be easy to miss the underlying gravity, and perhaps the avant-garde will find Anderson's pictures too accessible. I hope not. Anderson is bound to be misunderstood, but then that's a large club for artists, and he is a genuine one.

After knowing Wes for a while – and being thankful that he is considerably film literate; in other words, that he has a clear sense of what has preceded him, also a rarity with directors these days – I quoted a line from a favourite picture of mine (and his, it turned out), applying the phrase to him. In Hawks' *Rio Bravo* (1959), John Wayne expresses to a friend his admiration for Ricky Nelson's youthful professionalism: 'It's nice to see a smart kid for a change.'

Peter Bogdanovich

The Royal Tenenbaums

CAST AND CREW

INSERT:

A first edition copy of The Royal Tenenbaums.

On the dust jacket there is an illustration of a cream-coloured note card that looks like a wedding invitation. The title of the book is engraved on the card.

The next page says Chapter One.

NARRATOR
Royal Tenenbaum bought the house on Archer Avenue in the winter of his thirty-fifth year.

CUT TO:

A five-storey limestone town house. A forty-three-year-old man in a raincoat rings the front doorbell. He is Royal.

NARRATOR
Over the next decade, he and his wife had three children, and then they separated.

INT. DINING ROOM. DAY

Royal sits at the head of a long table. He is surrounded by his children.

Chas is twelve, with curly hair, dressed in a black suit and a tie. Margot is ten, with a barrette in her hair, wearing a knitted Lacoste dress and penny loafers. Richie is eight, with long hair, parted on the side, dressed in a Bjorn Borg-style tennis outfit and a headband.

Chas wears a blank expression, Margot looks as if she is about to cry, and Richie has tears all over his face.

MARGOT

Are you getting divorced?

ROYAL
(gently)

At the moment, no. But it doesn't look good.

RICHIE

Do you still love us?

ROYAL

Of course, I do.

CHAS
(*pointedly*)

Do you still love Mom?

ROYAL

Very much. But she asked me to leave, and I had to respect her position on the matter.

MARGOT

Was it our fault?

ROYAL
(*long pause*)

No. Obviously, we had to make certain sacrifices as a result of having children, but no. Lord, no.

RICHIE

Why'd she ask you to leave?

ROYAL
(*sadly*)

I don't really know any more. Maybe I wasn't as true to her as I could've been.

CHAS

Well, she says –

ROYAL

Let's not rehash it, Chassie.

An Indian man with salt-and-pepper hair, dressed in pink pants, a white shirt and a white apron, comes in from the kitchen with a Martini on a tray. He is Pagoda.

NARRATOR

They were never legally divorced.

Pagoda hands Royal the Martini.

ROYAL

Thanks, Pagoda.

INT. HALLWAY. DAY

A gallery of the children's art, done mostly in crayon, but with beautiful frames and careful lighting. The subject matter includes:

spaceships, wild animals, sailboats, motorcycles, and war scenes with tanks and paratroopers.

A stuffed and mounted boar's head with its teeth bared hangs in the stairwell. A label on it says Wild Javelina, Andes Mountains. Under the stairs there is a telephone room the size of a closet. Old messages are tacked to the walls, and children's heights are marked on the door frame.

A thirty-three-year-old woman with a scarf around her neck and sunglasses on top of her head talks on a rotary telephone. She is Etheline. Richie sits on her lap reading an Atlas of the World. *Margot sits on a footstool reading* The Cherry Orchard. *Chas stands in the doorway with a slip of blue paper in his hand.*

NARRATOR
Etheline Tenenbaum kept the house and raised the children, and their education was her highest priority.

Etheline says into the telephone:

ETHELINE
I'll hold, thank you.

CHAS
I need $187.

ETHELINE
(pause)
Write yourself a cheque.

Chas hands Etheline the slip of blue paper.

INSERT:

A cheque made out in the amount of $187. Etheline signs it.

CUT TO:

Chas taking back the cheque. Etheline says into the telephone:

ETHELINE
Bene. Si. Grazie mille.

Etheline hangs up. There is a schedule of activities – guitar, ballet, yoga, scuba-diving – written on a chalkboard behind her and divided into columns labelled Chas, Richie and Margot. She changes an Italian lesson from 4.30 to 5.30.

NARRATOR
She wrote a book on the subject.

INSERT:

A copy of Etheline Tenenbaum's book, Family of Geniuses. *On the dust jacket there is a photograph of the three children conducting a press conference in a room crowded with journalists. It appears to have been published in the late seventies.*

CUT TO:

The press conference. Chas points to a reporter.

CHAS
The gentleman in the blue cardigan, please.

REPORTER
Thank you. I have a two-part question.

CHAS
Go ahead.

INT. CHAS' BEDROOM. DAY

Chas' room looks like a businessman's office, except it is very small and has bunk beds. There is a desk with an Apple II computer and an electric coffee pot on it. There is a water cooler in the corner, with a paper cup dispenser.

Chas stands talking on the telephone while Etheline brings in his lunch on a tray.

NARRATOR
Chas Tenenbaum had, since elementary school, taken most of his meals in his room, standing up at his desk with a cup of coffee, to save time.

On a shelf in an alcove there are ten cages connected together by plastic tubes. White mice with tiny black spots all over them race around inside the cages. Chas feeds one of them a drop of blue liquid from a test tube.

NARRATOR
In the sixth grade, he went into business, breeding dalmatian mice, which he sold to a pet shop in Little Tokyo.

There are twenty-five pinstriped suits in boys' size twelve and an electric tie rack hanging in the closet. Chas pushes a button on the tie rack and the ties glide along a track.

NARRATOR
He started buying real estate in his early teens and seemed to have an almost preternatural understanding of international finance.

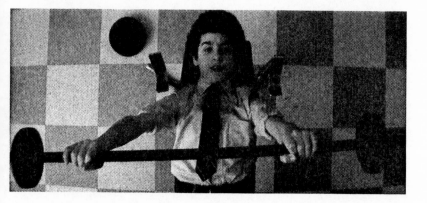

There are a small weightlifting bench and a punchbag in the corner. There is a set of exercise charts neatly drawn with felt-tip pen tacked to the wall. Chas bench-presses about fifty pounds on a small barbell.

NARRATOR
He negotiated the purchase of his father's summer house on Eagle's Island.

EXT. BACKYARD. DAY

A house in the country. Chas crouches in the bushes with a B.B. gun. Across the lawn he sees two younger boys with B.B. guns drop down from a tree. One of the boys is Richie, and the other has nearly-white blond hair. He is Eli. He wears Apache warpaint.

Chas gets Richie in his sights.

ROYAL

Hold it, Chassie.

Chas freezes. He looks up and sees Royal watching from the roof with a B.B. gun trained on him. Royal is dressed in khaki pants, sunglasses, and no shirt.

CHAS

What are you doing? You're on my team!

ROYAL
(*hesitates*)

There are no teams.

Royal fires. Chas screams and fires back as Royal scrambles away, laughing.

NARRATOR

The B.B. was still lodged between two knuckles in Chas' left hand.

INT. MARGOT'S BEDROOM. DAY

The walls of Margot's room are red, with little running zebras painted all over them. There is a collection of African masks hanging in the corner. Margot sits at a small metal stand, typing on an I.B.M. typewriter.

NARRATOR

Margot Tenenbaum was adopted at age two. Her father had always noted this when introducing her.

CUT TO:

A cocktail party. Royal introduces Margot to a group of elderly men in black tie.

ROYAL

This is my adopted daughter, Margot Tenenbaum.

Margot nods politely.

CUT TO:

A wall filled with bookshelves. There are thousands of books of plays. Margot takes out a copy of The Iceman Cometh.

NARRATOR
She was a playwright and won a Braverman Grant of fifty thousand dollars in the ninth grade.

There is mock-up of a stage set for a play that appears to have taken place in a network of tree houses on a tropical island. Margot places a tiny canoe beneath a palm tree.

NARRATOR
She and her brother Richie ran away from home one winter and camped out in the African Wing of the Public Archives.

EXT. MUSEUM. DAY

Richie and Margot sit on a bench in front of a large Gothic building. Richie has on a backpack with a sleeping bag attached to it. Margot carries a small red suitcase. They both look extremely dishevelled and tired.

A single-file line of students in Catholic school uniforms goes past them following a museum guide. Eli is at the end of the line. He stops and stares at Margot and Richie.

RICHIE
Hi, Eli.

ELI
You said I could run away, too.

MARGOT
No, I didn't. And don't tell anybody you saw us.

CUT TO:

Richie and Margot sharing a Boy Scout sleeping bag on a bench in a gallery of wildlife dioramas in the darkened museum. Margot reads a book about sharks by the light of a flashlight. Richie is asleep.

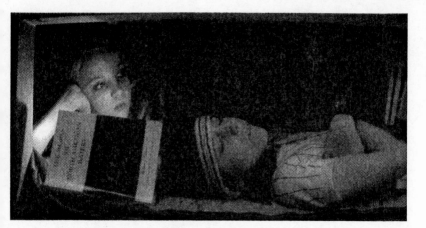

NARRATOR
Four years later, she disappeared alone for two weeks and came back with half a finger missing.

INSERT:

A pair of knitted gloves. One finger has been clipped off at the middle knuckle and is being sewn up.

INT. RICHIE'S BEDROOM. DAY

Richie's room is in the attic. There are a chemistry set, a drum set and a long shelf filled with tennis trophies. Richie sits on the edge of his bed.

NARRATOR
Richie Tenenbaum had been a champion tennis player since the third grade.

There are thousands of Matchbox cars arranged on every available inch of space on tables, desks and window sills. Richie parks a little Mazerati next to a dune buggy.

NARRATOR
He turned pro at seventeen and won the U.S. Nationals three years in a row.

There is a ham radio set in the corner of the room. Richie sits at the console wearing a set of headphones. There is a map of the world on the wall, with coloured pins stuck in different cities.

NARRATOR

He kept a studio in the corner of the ballroom but had
failed to develop as a painter.

CUT TO:

*A ballroom with vaulted ceilings and a giant chandelier on the top
floor of the house. One corner is filled with seventeen almost identical
portraits of Margot looking over the top of a book with an irritated
expression. Etheline helps Richie hang a new portrait among the
others.*

NARRATOR

On weekends, Royal took him on outings around the city.

EXT. STREET. DAY

*Royal and Richie stand among a group of Puerto Rican men as two
large, vicious-looking pit bulls with scars all over them snarl at each
other. Royal yells along with the others:*

ROYAL

Vamanos! Andale!

*Royal throws a fifty-dollar bill into a pile of money on the sidewalk.
Richie throws in a dollar.*

These invitations were never extended to anyone else.

CUT TO:

The second floor of the Tenenbaum house. Chas sits alone in one window. Margot sits alone in the next. They both watch as Royal and Richie get out of a gypsy cab in front of the house, sharing a bag of peanuts and laughing.

There is a slightly run-down thirty-five-storey apartment building across the street. Eli sits alone in a window.

INT. APARTMENT. DAY

A two-room apartment with a crucifix on the wall. Eli finishes making his bed and folds it into the couch. An elderly woman works at a sewing machine in the next room.

NARRATOR
Richie's best friend Eli Cash lived with his aunt in a building across the street.

EXT. STREET. DAY

Eli walks up the front steps of the Tenenbaum house and rings the doorbell. He wears a set of house keys on a string around his neck. Pagoda opens the door. He is dressed in pyjamas, slippers and a bathrobe. He lets Eli inside.

NARRATOR
He was a regular fixture at family gatherings, holidays, mornings before school and most afternoons.

CUT TO:

The Tenenbaum house at night. There are strings of coloured lights glowing around the front door and white paper bags with candles in them on the steps. Royal rings the front doorbell. He carries a small package wrapped in red-and-pink-striped paper with a white ribbon on it.

NARRATOR

The three Tenenbaum children performed Margot's first play on the night of her eleventh birthday.

INT. BALLROOM. NIGHT

There are twenty eleven-year-olds wearing party hats. Margot, Chas and Richie are in costumes. Margot is a zebra, Chas is a bear and Richie is a leopard. Eli is dressed in pyjamas. Royal sits at a table with them, drinking a glass of whiskey.

NARRATOR

They had agreed to invite their father to the party.

There is a small stage-set across the room for a play that appears to have taken place on a ship.

CHAS

What'd you think, Dad?

ROYAL

It didn't seem believable to me.

Chas looks to Margot. She is silent. Royal says to Eli:

ROYAL

Why are you wearing pyjamas? Do you live here?

RICHIE

He has permission to sleep over.

Royal shakes his head.

CHAS

Did you think the characters were –

ROYAL

What characters? It was just a bunch of little kids dressed in animal costumes.

MARGOT

Goodnight, everyone.

Margot quickly collects her unopened presents from the table. She puts Royal's aside and sets it in front of him.

ROYAL

Sweetie. Don't get mad at me. That's just one man's opinion.

The lights go down. Royal looks across the room. Etheline stands in the doorway with a birthday cake on a tray. The candles are lit. She looks furious. Pagoda stands at the light switch. Everyone begins to sing Happy Birthday. Margot walks out of the room, and the singing disintegrates.

NARRATOR

He had not been invited to any of their parties since.

Etheline blows out the candles.

EXT. ROOF. DAY

There is a large antenna for Richie's ham radio and a wooden coop with a falcon in it. The falcon has a hood over its eyes. Richie opens the coop, carefully removes the falcon's hood, and feeds him some sardines from a tin.

NARRATOR

In fact, virtually all memory of the brilliance of the young Tenenbaums had been erased by two decades of betrayal, failure and disaster.

Richie carries the falcon on his arm to the edge of the roof.

RICHIE

Go, Mordecai.

The falcon spreads its wings and lunges into the sky.

MONTAGE:

(The names of each of our characters and the names of the actors playing them appear over the following shots.)

Royal Tenenbaum sits in a chair in his hotel suite with no shirt on and a towel wrapped around his face. A woman in a white apron lifts off the towel, and Royal looks in the mirror. He is now sixty-six, with grey hair, white at the temples, worn very long in the back. He is getting a facial, and there are strips of blue cellophane covering his face. The

woman quickly peels them away and begins to massage his temples.
Royal lights a cigarette at the end of a three-inch holder.

Etheline Tenenbaum draws eyeliner around her eyes in her dressing
mirror. She is fifty-five and has long, black hair with one silver streak
that runs through it. She wears a pink slip and a gold locket. The wall
behind her is filled with portraits of tribesmen and native warriors
from around the world. She holds up a pair of prescription sunglasses
and looks at herself. She lowers them and does her lipstick.

Chas Tenenbaum shaves in the locker room of a boxing gym. Steam
fills the air. He is thirty-six and in top fighting condition. Ari and Uzi
Tenenbaum are on either side of him. They are eight and ten. They are
also shaving, but with no blades in their razors. All three have
extremely curly black hair.

Margot Tenenbaum is at the hairdresser's with three people working on
her at once. She is thirty-four. Her hair is being dyed, and there are
little clamps and bits of foil twisted into it. She is smoking a cigarette,
and she blows a puff of smoke as the hair dryer is lowered onto her
head. She holds an open copy of a book of plays by George Bernard
Shaw. She has one fake finger made of wood.

Eli Cash is in the fitting room of a clothing store having a white
buckskin jacket with fringe taken in. A tailor pulls at the hem of the
jacket and sticks pins in the sleeves. The tailor's helper brings Eli a
cup of tea and some cucumber sandwiches. Eli picks out a sandwich.
A second helper hands him a short-brimmed Stetson cowboy hat.
He puts it on at an angle and stares at himself.

Raleigh St. Clair brushes his teeth with an electric toothbrush in a
very small, white-tiled bathroom. He has a full, grey beard and round
glasses, and he is dressed in red silk pyjamas with white piping. He
stops suddenly, picks up a tape recorder off the edge of the sink, and
excitedly dictates something into it. He puts the tape recorder back on
the sink and starts brushing his teeth again.

Henry Sherman stands in front of a mirrored wall in the vestibule
of his building. He is a tall, black man, fifty-six years old, with grey
hair and a moustache. He wears a double-breasted navy blazer. He
carefully folds a chequered handkerchief and tucks it into his breast
pocket. There is a hand-lettered sign regarding trash and recycling

taped to the wall behind him, underneath a row of mailboxes. It is signed H. Sherman, the Landlord, in red ink.

Richie Tenenbaum looks at himself in the mirror in his stateroom on board an ocean liner. He is thirty-two, with long hair, parted on the side, and a beard. He wears a khaki suit, a striped tennis shirt, a headband, and penny loafers. The ocean goes by at a fast clip in the porthole behind him. A towel on the dresser says The Côte d'Ivoire in red stitching. He takes out a little camera. He points it at his reflection, smiles sadly, and takes a picture of himself. He puts the camera back into his pocket and goes out the door.

INSERT:

Page 22 of The Royal Tenenbaums. *It says Chapter Two.*

INT. HOTEL ROOM. DAY

Royal's suite at the Lindbergh Palace Hotel. There are shelves full of law books and hundreds of spy novels in stacks on the floor. There is a set of Encyclopedia Britannica, *an exercise bicycle and a Xerox machine.*

Royal lies on his stomach on a massage table getting a massage from a young Asian woman. The manager of the hotel stands in front of Royal with a piece of paper in his hand.

> MANAGER
> I've been instructed to refuse any further charges on your room account and to direct you in writing to, please, vacate the premises by the end of the month.

The manager hands Royal the piece of paper. Royal points to the masseuse.

> ROYAL
> What about Sing-Sang? I owe her a hundred.

The manager looks to the masseuse.

> NARRATOR
> Royal had lived in the Lindbergh Palace Hotel for twenty-two years.

A letter typed on Lindbergh Palace Hotel stationery. It begins:

> Dear Mr Tenenbaum,
> In light of your continuing failure to remit any form of
> payment, we have no –

CUT TO:

The masseuse. She does not appear to understand English.

>   MANAGER
> Can you pay her in cash?

Royal shakes his head. The manager hesitates.

>   NARRATOR
> He was a prominent litigator until the mid-eighties, when
> he was disbarred and briefly imprisoned.

CUT TO:

*Royal standing in the window looking out at the falling snow as Sing-
Sang folds up the massage table behind him. He lights a cigarette.*

>   NARRATOR
> No one in his family had spoken to him in three years.

INT. RADIO ROOM. DAY

The radio room on board the Côte d'Ivoire. *There are computer
terminals, short-wave radios, maps on the walls, and a crew of
technicians in white uniforms. There is a mist outside the window,
and an oil tanker in the distance.*

*The radio operator finishes typing a message into a keyboard and
looks up to Richie.*

>   RICHIE
> Read it back to me so far, Pietro.

>   RADIO OPERATOR
> Dear Eli, I'm in the middle of the ocean. I haven't left my
> room in four days. I've never been more lonely in my life,
> and I think I'm in love with Margot.

The radio operator looks to Richie. Richie nods.

RICHIE
New paragraph.

Richie takes a sip of a Bloody Mary.

NARRATOR
Richie had retired from professional tennis at twenty-six.
His last match had been widely discussed in the media.

INSERT:

A copy of the Sporting Press *magazine. On the cover there is a
photograph of Richie standing at the baseline of a tennis court. He
wears no shoes and only one sock, and there are tears all over his face.
The stands behind him are filled with confused fans. A caption across
the page says: Meltdown!' and, in smaller letters, Tenenbaum suffers
mid-match nervous collapse in the semis at Windswept Fields.*

CUT TO:

Richie dictating to the radio operator.

RICHIE
Your friend, Richie. End of letter.

*Richie signs a slip of paper and hands it to the radio operator. He
wraps a scarf around his neck and goes out the door.*

NARRATOR
For the past year he had been travelling alone on an ocean
liner called the *Côte d'Ivoire* and had seen both poles, five
oceans, the Amazon and the Nile.

INT. LIBRARY. NIGHT

*Eli stands at a podium reading from a book to a crowded audience.
A telegram marked Ship to Shore is tucked into his coat pocket. His
voice is quietly dramatic.*

ELI
The crickets and the rust-beetles scuttled among the nettles
of the sagethicket. Vamanos, amigos, he whispered, and threw

the busted leather flintcraw over the loose weave of the
saddlecock. And they rode on in the friscalating dusklight.

Eli looks up. He closes his book. The audience applauds uproariously.

NARRATOR
Eli was an assistant professor of English Literature at Brooks
College. The recent publication of his second novel –

INSERT:

A copy of Eli Cash's latest book, Old Custer. *On the dust jacket there
is an illustration of an Indian in warpaint with a long, bloody knife
clasped between his teeth and a yellow scalp hanging from his hand.*

INT. LOBBY. NIGHT

*Eli walks among the card catalogues surrounded by a crowd of
admirers.*

NARRATOR
– had earned him a sudden, unexpected literary celebrity.

CUT TO:

*Eli standing near the circulation desk with a group of professors
drinking cocktails.*

ELI
Well, everyone knows Custer died at Little Bighorn. What
this book presupposes is: (*tentatively*) maybe he didn't?

Eli shrugs and smiles.

CUT TO:

*Eli placing a call from a payphone in the lobby. He unfolds a
newspaper clipping and looks at it while he waits. He says suddenly
into the receiver:*

ELI
Let me ask you something. Why would a review make the
point of saying someone's not a genius? I mean, do you
think I'm especially not a genius? Isn't that –

Someone gives Eli a book to sign. He scribbles his name on it and hands it back without looking. He says sadly:

ELI

You didn't even have to think about it, did you?

INT. BATHROOM. NIGHT

The bathroom of Margot and Raleigh's apartment. Margot sits Indian-style on the counter painting her toenails red and talking on the telephone. There are cotton balls in between her toes, and she has a towel wrapped around her.

Hot water runs full blast in the bathtub. A little black-and-white television set is tuned in to the six o'clock news with the sound turned off. Margot whispers into the telephone:

MARGOT

Well, I just don't use that word lightly.

Margot takes a drag of a cigarette balanced at the edge of the sink. There is a knock on the door. Margot does not look up.

MARGOT

I have to go, Eli.

Margot hangs up the telephone. There is another knock.

RALEIGH

Margot?

Raleigh has an English accent with a lisp. Margot answers without taking the cigarette out of her mouth:

MARGOT

Uh-huh?

RALEIGH

May I come in, please?

Margot puts out her cigarette. She waves the smoke away, turns on a little electric fan, and sprays perfume into the air with an atomizer. She reaches over and unlocks the door with her foot.

Raleigh cracks open the door and looks inside. He is wearing red pyjamas and a camel's-hair bathrobe. He seems worried and intimidated.

NARRATOR

Margot was married to the writer and neurologist Raleigh St. Clair.

INSERT:

A copy of Raleigh St. Clair's latest book, The Peculiar Neurodegenerative Inhabitants of the Kazawa Atoll. *On the dust jacket there is a photograph of Raleigh – dressed in a speedo, with goggles on top of his head – on a beach, standing next to a Kazawa. The Kazawa stares at him curiously.*

CUT TO:

Raleigh looking in the bathroom doorway.

RALEIGH

How are you, my darling?

MARGOT

Fine, thank you.

Margot blows on her toenails.

RALEIGH

You must eat something. Shall I make your dinner?

MARGOT

No, thank you.

Margot taps her fingers on the counter. The wooden one makes a clicking sound. She looks to Raleigh. Raleigh hesitates. He goes out suddenly and closes the door. Margot reaches over with her foot and locks it.

NARRATOR

She was known for her extreme secrecy. For example, none of the Tenenbaums knew she was a smoker, which she had been since the age of twelve.

Margot opens a box of Q-Tips. There is a cigarette hidden inside. She takes it out and lights it.

NARRATOR

Nor were they aware of her first marriage and divorce to a recording artist in Jamaica.

INSERT:

A remaindered copy of Desmond Winston Manchester XI's L.P. record Dynamite Stick. On the sleeve there is a photograph of five Rastafarians standing in front of a metal shack. A younger Margot stands behind them partly hidden in the door frame. She is dressed in a string bikini.

NARRATOR

She kept a private studio in Mockingbird Heights under the name Helen Scott.

INT. STUDIO. DAY

A small room with one wooden chair and a metal stand with an I.B.M. electric typewriter on it. There are posters for several of Margot's plays leaning against the walls. The titles include: Static Electricity, Erotic Transference *and* Nakedness Tonight.

NARRATOR

She had not completed a play in seven years.

INT. RALEIGH'S LABORATORY. DAY

Raleigh's basement. Raleigh sits at a table, across from a fifteen-year-old boy in a plaid fishing hat with Dudley stitched across the front. Raleigh is dressed in a turtleneck shirt and a corduroy blazer with suede patches on the elbows. The boy has an earphone in his ear. He wears Henry Aaron-style flip-up sunglasses.

Raleigh and Dudley both have a set of building blocks in front of them. Raleigh's are arranged in the shape of a symmetrical cross. Dudley's are strewn out randomly. A cardboard screen stands in between the two sets of blocks.

Raleigh says into his tape recorder:

RALEIGH

Seventeen October. Third examination of Dudley
Heinsbergen.

Raleigh lifts the cardboard screen and looks to Dudley.

RALEIGH

All right, Dudley. Make yours look like mine.

Dudley sets to work, moving his blocks around slowly.

NARRATOR

Raleigh's next book was on the subject of a condition he
called Heinsbergen's Syndrome.

*Dudley finishes arranging his blocks into the shape of a lop-sided
octagon with branches coming out of it.*

DUDLEY

Done.

Raleigh begins to laugh quietly. He shakes his head.

RALEIGH

My goodness. How interesting. How bizarre.

CUT TO:

*Raleigh sitting in a corner. Dudley stands on the far side of the room
misspelling words on a chalkboard. Raleigh whispers into his tape
recorder:*

RALEIGH

Dudley suffers from a rare disorder combining the symptoms
of amnesia, dyslexia and colour-blindness, with a highly
acute sense of hearing.

Dudley turns around suddenly and frowns.

RALEIGH

There is also evidence of –

DUDLEY

I'm not colour-blind, am I?

Raleigh looks to Dudley. He hesitates.

I'm afraid you are.

INT. CHAS' APARTMENT. NIGHT

Ari and Uzi's bedroom. It is perfectly neat and organized like a military barracks. There are night lights in every socket. There are two fire extinguishers and a large first-aid kit mounted on the wall. There is a turtle in a fish tank in the corner. Ari and Uzi are sound asleep in their bunk beds.

Chas stands in the doorway. His expression is blank. In one hand, he holds a small tape recorder. In the other hand, he holds a fishing lantern.

He turns on the lantern, which begins blinking rapidly in a strobe effect. He presses play on the tape recorder, which blasts a recording of a police siren at full volume. He yells at the top of his lungs:

CHAS
Fire alarm! Ari! Uzi! Let's go! Look alive!

Ari bolts out of the top bunk. He is shirtless and has on pyjama bottoms. He puts on a pair of cleats and grabs the turtle out of the fish tank. Uzi sits up. He looks half asleep. Chas runs around the room, tipping over chairs and blasting the tape recorder. He looks to Uzi. He screams:

CHAS
Uzi! Let's go!

INT. HALLWAY. NIGHT

Ari presses the button for the elevator and waits. The apartment is extremely large and spare. It looks like a museum.

NARRATOR
Chas' wife, Rachael, was killed in a plane crash the previous summer.

Chas and Uzi rush into the hallway. Uzi has on a pajama top and underwear. Chas yells to Ari:

26

CHAS

No elevators! There's a fire!

INT. STAIRWELL. NIGHT

They race down the stairs. Chas picks up Uzi.

UZI

What about Buckley?

CHAS

You forgot him.

Uzi starts to cry.

INSERT:

A slide projected onto a screen. Ari and Uzi and their mother stand in front of a small plane outside a hangar. The mother has on sunglasses, with a scarf tied over her hair. The wind blows her dress sideways, and she is laughing. The boys wear camp shorts and no shirts. Uzi is doing a karate stance.

There is a beagle looking out of the window of the plane.

NARRATOR

Chas and their two sons, Ari and Uzi, were also on the flight, and survived, as did their dog, who was discovered in his cage several thousand yards from the crash site.

CUT TO:

A dog's cage upside down in the desert surrounded by scraps of metal and clothing. A cloud of smoke billows in the distance.

INT. BATHROOM. NIGHT

The beagle is asleep next to the bathtub on a little bed with Buckley written on it. He looks very old and has white fur around his eyes. His breathing is wheezy. Chas' siren can be heard in the distance outside the window. It stops.

EXT. SIDEWALK. NIGHT

Chas, Ari and Uzi stand on the sidewalk, looking up at the building. The street is deserted. The tape recorder has been turned off. The lantern is still blinking.

Chas turns off the lantern and presses stop on his stopwatch.

> CHAS
> Four minutes and forty-eight seconds. We're all dead. Burned to a crisp.

Chas shakes his head. He looks disoriented and weak.

> NARRATOR
> Over the last six months, he had become increasingly concerned with their safety.

Uzi is still crying.

> UZI
> We left Buckley.

Chas rubs his eyes and his temples. He says quietly:

> CHAS
> It doesn't matter.

Chas sits down on the sidewalk. Ari and Uzi look scared. The doorman watches uneasily from the lobby.

INT. ETHELINE'S STUDY. DAY

The walls of Etheline's study are filled with pre-Columbian art and primitive tools and weapons. There are shelves full of hundreds of bones and bits of pottery with little numbers painted on them. There are stacks of National Geographics *on the floor. A human skeleton hangs on a stand in the corner.*

> NARRATOR
> Etheline became an archaeologist and had overseen excavations for the Department of Housing and the Transit Authority.

The back doors are open on to the garden. Pagoda sits on a bench outside, peeling potatoes, listening to a Walkman with headphones. His hair is now white.

Etheline is at her desk studying an arrowhead while Henry sits next to her. He is working on her taxes.

HENRY

Apropos of my question re: I–40 slash I–9 adjustments.

Henry stands up. He seems very nervous. Etheline looks up at him curiously.

NARRATOR

She taught a bridge class twice a week with her friend and business manager, Henry Sherman.

INSERT:

A copy of Henry Sherman's book, Accounting for Everything. *A caption at the top of the cover says* A Guide to Personal Finance. *It appears to have been published in the late sixties.*

CUT TO:

Henry looking down at Etheline.

HENRY

It would probably be advantageous for your marital status to be legally established as single, in light of the circumstances.

ETHELINE

What do you mean?

HENRY

I mean for tax purposes.

ETHELINE
(*pause*)

But I thought it was –

HENRY

Etheline?

ETHELINE

Yes?

HENRY

Will you marry me?

Pagoda stops peeling the potatoes. He takes off one ear of his headphones. Etheline puts on her prescription sunglasses.

HENRY

I love you. Did you already know that?

ETHELINE

No, I didn't.

Henry nods calmly.

NARRATOR

Since her separation from her husband, she had had many suitors –

MONTÁGE:

A large man stands on a glacier in Antarctica with penguins behind him. He wears a hooded fur coat and has ice frozen into his beard. He checks the elevation with a compass. A title identifies him as Neville Smythe-Dorléac.

NEVILLE SMYTHE-DORLEAC

An Asian man in a tweed suit and large, perfectly round glasses sits on a settee in a room filled with avant-garde furniture and sculpture.

He has several sets of blueprints under his arm. A title identifies him as Yasuo Oshima.

A white-haired man sits in a director's chair on a sound stage, surrounded by extras dressed as futuristic earthlings and aliens. He has a strong, weathered face and wears a safari jacket. A title identifies him as Franklin Benedict.

CUT TO:

Henry looking down at Etheline. He has two bandaged shaving cuts, and a safety pin holds his glasses together.

> NARRATOR
> – but had not considered a single one until this moment.

Etheline starts to say something. She hesitates.

> ETHELINE
> This isn't really a tax issue, is it?

> HENRY
> (*pause*)
> That's true. I don't know why I put it that way.

Etheline smiles slightly. She takes Henry's hand.

> ETHELINE
> Let me think about it, Henry.

Pagoda frowns.

INT. TELEPHONE ROOM. DAY

Pagoda places a call.

> PAGODA
> Hello, please. Tell Mr Royal this is the Pagoda.

INT. ELEVATOR. DAY

Royal rides down in the elevator at the Lindbergh Palace. He is dressed in a grey double-breasted Savile Row pinstripe suit, a dark pink shirt, a red-and-pink-striped tie, and Aristotle Onassis-style wrap-around sunglasses. He smokes a cigarette.

The elevator operator has a thin, grey moustache and jet-black hair. He is Dusty. The elevator stops.

ROYAL

Thanks, Dusty.

DUSTY

You're welcome.

INT. LOBBY. DAY

The elevator doors open and Royal strides out quickly. He crosses through the gigantic lobby. A bellboy appears.

BELLBOY

There's a call for you, Mr Tenenbaum.

ROYAL

Who is it?

BELLBOY

A Mr Pagoda.

ROYAL

I'll take it in there.

Royal points to a little wood-panelled telephone booth.

INT. TELEPHONE BOOTH. DAY

The telephone rings. Royal answers it.

ROYAL

What do you got?

EXT. CITY PARK. DAY

Royal and Pagoda stand alone in the middle of a field. A light, misting rain falls.

PAGODA

The black man asks her to be his wife.

ROYAL
(*quietly*)
No shit? And what'd Ethel say?

32

She thinks about it.

Royal stares off into space. He shakes his head.

ROYAL

I don't like the sound of this one damn bit, Pagoda. I mean, Lord knows I've had my share of infidelities. But she's still my wife. (*Pause.*) And no goddamn two-bit chartered accountant's going to change that.

INSERT:

Page 50 of The Royal Tenenbaums. *It says Chapter Three.*

INT. HALLWAY. NIGHT

The doorbell rings. Pagoda comes into the hallway and opens the front door. Uzi is on the steps with a duffel bag over his shoulder and a stack of colouring books under his arm. Buckley is at his side. Buckley has a cold and coughs often.

There is a silver B.M.W. parked at the kerb with three doors and the trunk open. Chas, Ari and a uniformed driver are unpacking suitcases, blankets, boxes, clothes, toys, boxing gloves and a computer. The driver is Anwar.

Chas, Ari and Uzi all wear red Adidas warm-ups.

CHAS

Give us a hand, Pagoda.

Pagoda frowns. He starts down the steps.

INT. LIVING ROOM. NIGHT

There are twenty people at five card tables playing bridge. Most of them are in their fifties and sixties. They look very distinguished. Etheline and Henry are among them.

Chas, Ari, Uzi, Anwar and Pagoda come out of the hallway and cross through the living room, struggling with all of their possessions. Pagoda carries the fish tank with the turtle in it. Buckley follows them.

The bridge players watch strangely as they pass. Chas looks back at them but keeps moving. Etheline hesitates.

                    ETHELINE

Chas?

Chas stops in the doorway. Pagoda leads Ari, Uzi, Anwar and Buckley out of the room, up the stairs.

                    ETHELINE

What's going on?

                    CHAS

We got locked out of our apartment.

Etheline seems confused.

                    ETHELINE

Did you call a locksmith?

                    CHAS
                 (*hesitates*)

Uh-huh.

                    ETHELINE
                  (*pause*)

I don't understand. Did you pack your bags before you got locked out? Or how did you –

                    CHAS

It's not safe over there.

Silence. Etheline looks to her guests.

                    ETHELINE

Excuse me for a moment, please.

INT. HALLWAY. NIGHT

Etheline closes the sliding door to the living room. She and Chas stand alone in the hallway.

                    ETHELINE

What are you talking about?

34

CHAS

The apartment. I have to get some new sprinklers and a
back-up security system installed.

ETHELINE

But there're no sprinklers here, either.

Chas looks up and studies the ceiling. He shrugs.

CHAS

Well, we might have to do something about that, too.

Etheline looks concerned.

CUT TO:

*Two dalmatian mice chewing on a plate of hors d'oevres on the
window sill. The bridge players watch them silently.*

INT. CHAS' BEDROOM. NIGHT

*Ari and Uzi sit silently on the bunk beds in Chas' room. They have
dark circles under their eyes and seem exhausted. Chas walks around
the room examining things. He looks like a wreck, but acts incredibly
cheerful, pretending not to notice how sad the boys look.*

CHAS

Isn't this great? It feels like we're camping.

Chas chuckles as he turns on his old electric tie rack.

ARI

When are we going home?

Chas sees something across the room. He frowns.

CHAS

Who put that in here?

*There is a framed poster leaning against the wall in the corner. It is
a tennis-shoe advertisement with a picture of Richie holding a trophy
over his head, surrounded by a cheering crowd. A caption across the
top says The Baumer. Chas turns it around to face the wall. He kisses
Ari and Uzi goodnight.*

CHAS

See you in the morning.

Chas goes out the door. A moment later, he comes back in.

CHAS

You know what? I'm going to sleep in here, and that way
we can all be together.

*Chas spreads out a blanket on the floor and lies down. Uzi comes over
and lies down next to him.*

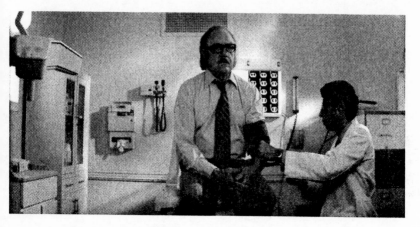

INT. DOCTOR'S OFFICE. DAY

*Royal sits on the edge of an examination table with white butcher
paper on it. A young doctor on a rolling stool takes Royal's blood
pressure as they talk.*

ROYAL

What kind of side effects can be expected?

DOCTOR

Well, there're a number of possibilities. Severe nausea and
dizziness are standard. A certain percentage of patients may
also experience seizure.

ROYAL

You mean like flopping around on the floor and everything?

DOCTOR

In some cases.

Royal nods gravely.

EXT. HALLWAY. DAY

Etheline and Raleigh stand outside the bathroom in Margot and Raleigh's apartment. Etheline has on an overcoat and gloves. Raleigh knocks on the door.

RALEIGH

You have a visitor, my darling.

Margot answers without opening the door:

MARGOT

Who is it?

ETHELINE

It's me, sweetie.

Silence. A key slides from under the door to Etheline's feet. Etheline looks to Raleigh. Raleigh looks embarrassed.

INT. BATHROOM. DAY

Margot is in the bathtub watching Planet of the Apes *on her little black-and-white television set. Etheline sits on the edge of the tub with her coat in her lap.*

ETHELINE

Raleigh says you've been spending six hours a day locked in here watching television and soaking in the tub.

MARGOT
(*pause*)

I doubt that.

ETHELINE

Well, I don't think that's very healthy, do you? Nor do I think it's very intelligent to keep an electrical gadget on the edge of the bathtub.

MARGOT

I tied it to the radiator.

Etheline examines the television set. There is a length of red twine wrapped around it and knotted to a pipe.

> ETHELINE

Well, it can't be very good for your eyes, anyway.

Margot turns off the television set with her foot. She looks to Etheline. Etheline smoothes back Margot's wet hair.

> ETHELINE

Chas came home.

> MARGOT
> (*pause*)

What do you mean?

> ETHELINE

He and Ari and Uzi are going to stay with me for a little while.

> MARGOT
> (*frowns*)

Why are they allowed to do that?

> ETHELINE
> (*hesitates*)

Well, I don't know, exactly. But I think he's been very depressed ever since –

> MARGOT
> (*urgently*)

So am I.

> ETHELINE
> (*pause*)

So are you what?

EXT. STREET. DAY

The front door of Margot and Raleigh's apartment building opens. Margot comes out and goes down the steps with three suitcases and her TV. Raleigh follows her. Etheline and Dudley walk behind them. Raleigh sounds desperately unhappy.

38

RALEIGH

But why is this bloody necessary?

MARGOT

Because I'm in a rut, and I need a change. Hang on.

Margot sets down her suitcases and goes into a telephone booth with graffiti spray-painted all over it. She closes the door and makes a call.

Etheline stands on the corner and raises her hand into the air. A gypsy cab pulls over. Raleigh waits uncomfortably outside the telephone booth. He watches Margot talking on the telephone. Dudley points at the taxi.

DUDLEY

That taxi has a dent in it.

Margot comes out of the telephone booth.

RALEIGH

You don't love me any more, do you?

MARGOT

I do, kind of. I can't explain it right now.

Raleigh looks crestfallen. Margot puts her suitcases into the back seat of the taxi. Dudley continues to point at it.

DUDLEY

Another dent here and another dent here.

MARGOT
(*gently*)

I'll call you, OK?

Raleigh nods. Margot gets into the taxi. Etheline looks at Raleigh sadly. She gets into the taxi and closes the door. Raleigh and Dudley watch the taxi drive away. Raleigh has tears in his eyes. Dudley takes a bite of a graham cracker.

INT. MARGOT'S BEDROOM. NIGHT

Margot goes into her room and sets her suitcases on the floor. She closes the door and locks it. She opens the door to the closet and turns on the light. She whispers:

MARGOT

Hello?

There is a rustle behind some hanging clothes. Eli looks out nervously and slowly emerges. He is dressed in white briefs. He whispers:

ELI

Hello, beautiful.

CUT TO:

Margot and Eli in Margot's single bed with the sheets pulled over their heads. Margot is eating potato chips, smoking a cigarette, and watching the news on her TV with the sound turned off.

ELI

Could we have dinner with your mother sometime?

Margot frowns. She looks at Eli strangely.

MARGOT

What for?

ELI
(shrugs)
I don't know. I'd just love to see her.

MARGOT

I don't think so, Eli.

Eli looks disappointed.

EXT. SIDEWALK. DAY

The next morning. Etheline comes out the front door of the Tenenbaum house and goes down the steps. Royal suddenly appears at her side.

ROYAL

You got a minute?

Etheline looks startled. She keeps walking.

ETHELINE

What are you doing here?

ROYAL

I need a favour. I want to spend some time with you and the children.

ETHELINE

Are you crazy?

ROYAL

Now, hold on, dammit.

ETHELINE

Stop following me.

ROYAL

I want my family back.

ETHELINE

Well, you can't have it. I'm sorry for you, but it's too late.

Royal hesitates for a fraction of a second.

ROYAL

I'm dying, baby.

Etheline stops. She looks to Royal.

ROYAL

I'm sick as a dog. I'll be dead in six weeks. I'm dying.

ETHELINE

What are you talking about?

Royal stares at her blankly. He nods.

ETHELINE

What happened?

Royal shrugs. Etheline looks stunned.

ETHELINE

Oh, my God.

Etheline looks as if she is going to faint. Royal seems suddenly worried.

ETHELINE

I'm sorry. I didn't know.

Etheline cannot seem to catch her breath. Royal looks around nervously.

ETHELINE

What'd they say? What's the prognosis?

Etheline begins to hyperventilate. Royal tries to calm her down.

ROYAL

Take it easy, Ethel.

Etheline stumbles a step and Royal catches her. He looks scared.

ROYAL

Hold on. Hold on.

ETHELINE
(*urgently*)
Where's the doctor? Let's get –

ROYAL

Wait a second.

Royal holds Etheline by the shoulders. He hesitates. He says gently, trying to comfort her:

ROYAL

Listen. I'm not dying. But I need some time.

Etheline looks puzzled.

ROYAL

A month. Maybe two. I want us to –

Etheline slaps Royal hard in the face. She says furiously:

ETHELINE

What's wrong with you?

ROYAL

Ethel.

ETHELINE

Go away!

Etheline turns away and walks quickly across the street.

ROYAL

Baby. I *am* dying.

Etheline stops. She looks back to Royal. She can see from the look on his face that now he is telling the truth. She goes over to him in the middle of the intersection.

ETHELINE

Are you or aren't you?

ROYAL
(*pause*)

Dying? Yes.

INT. HENRY'S APARTMENT/ETHELINE'S TELEPHONE ROOM. DAY

A telephone conversation. Henry sits at a desk in his study. There are ledger books and adding machines in front of him and glass statues of birds and animals behind him. Etheline is in the telephone room on Archer Avenue.

HENRY

Have you told your children?

ETHELINE

More or less.

HENRY

And are they all right?

ETHELINE

Hard to say.

INT. 375TH STREET Y/CHAS' ROOM. DAY

A second telephone conversation. Ari talks on a payphone next to an indoor pool. Uzi stands beside him. Each wears goggles and an orange life-jacket belted tightly. A sign on the wall says Water Safety and Rescue Class, 11 a.m. Chas sits at the desk in his bedroom on Archer Avenue.

UZI

Who's your father?

CHAS

His name's Royal Tenenbaum.

ARI

You told us he was already dead.

CHAS

(*hesitates*)

But now he's really dying.

INT. ELI'S CAR/MARGOT'S BATHROOM-DARKROOM. DAY

A third telephone conversation. Eli sits on a couch in front of a painting of two men wearing ski masks riding a motorcycle chasing after a screaming girl in a bikini. He smokes a long, Moroccan-looking pipe. Margot talks on the telephone in her bathroom on Archer Avenue. There are three bottles of developing chemicals and a photographic enlarger next to the sink.

ELI

I'm very sorry, Margot.

MARGOT

That's OK. We're not actually related, anyway.

ELI

That's true.

EXT. BOAT DECK. DAY

The Côte d'Ivoire. *Richie sits under a wool blanket in a chaise longue reading a telegram with Shore to Ship printed across the top. He looks upset. A waiter stands next to him with a pen and a pad of paper in his hand. All of the other passengers on the deck are very elderly and have white hair.*

RICHIE

I'd like to send a response, Alberto.

WAITER

Yes, sir. Go ahead.

RICHIE

Dear Mom, I received your message. I'm coming home as soon as possible. (*Pause.*) Who do I see about that?

44

The waiter shrugs.

The entrance to the passenger terminal for the Côte d'Ivoire. *A sign across the glass says Royal Arctic Line. Richie stands on the sidewalk with his hands in his pockets as bundled-up, white-haired passengers and baggage handlers rush by around him. He has two small suitcases and a vinyl bag with a pouch on the side for a tennis racquet. There is no racquet in it. Two elderly men with white hair come over to him.*

                    ELDERLY MAN I
    Can we get a picture with you, Baumer?

Richie nods. One of the elderly men gives his camera to a baggage handler, and they stand next to Richie.

                    ELDERLY MAN 2
    I saw you whip Vishniac in the finals at Glenchester. You
    were beautiful back then.

Richie smiles briefly. The baggage handler takes the picture.

                    ELDERLY MAN I
    Thanks, Champ.

The two elderly men walk away. A city bus stops at the corner. The door opens and Margot gets out. She smiles at Richie and waves. She wears a mink coat with a belt around it. She has on pink gloves. She walks across the sidewalk and stops ten feet in front of Richie as the bus drives away. They stand there smiling at each other.

                    MARGOT
    Stand up straight and let me get a look at you.

Richie stands up a little straighter and continues to look at Margot with the same smile.

                    MARGOT
    What's so funny?

Richie shrugs.

                    MARGOT
    Well, it's nice to see you, too.

45

Their smiles fade, and they look both cold and sad. Richie reaches out his hand. Margot goes over to him and puts her arms around him.

EXT. TENENBAUM HOUSE. DAY

Margot and Richie stand on the steps in front of the house. The door opens and Etheline and Pagoda come outside and hug Richie. Richie and Henry shake hands. Ari and Uzi come running out the door to hug Richie.

NARRATOR

That night, Etheline found all of her children living together under the same roof for the first time in seventeen years.

Chas watches from his window on the third floor. Richie looks up and sees him. Richie waves tentatively. Chas waves back without smiling.

EXT. ROOF. DAWN

Richie comes out on to the roof dressed in pyjamas. He opens his falcon's coop. He puts his hand under the falcon's feet, and the falcon steps on to his fist. The falcon's hood says Mordecai across the front. Richie pulls a leather cord and lifts the hood off the falcon's head. He strokes the falcon's feathers and talks softly in its ear.

NARRATOR

The next morning Richie woke at dawn. He had decided birds should not be kept in cages, fed Mordecai three sardines, and set him free.

CUT TO:

An hour later. Richie sits on a box on the roof eating a bowl of cereal and reading a book called Three Plays by Margot Tenenbaum. *There is an empty tin of sardines at his feet. The door to the falcon's coop is open, and the falcon is gone.*

INSERT:

Page 76 of The Royal Tenenbaums. *It says Chapter Four.*

EXT. STREET. EVENING

Royal gets out of a gypsy cab in front of the Tenenbaum house. He is dressed in a white bathrobe, white pyjamas, and red bedroom slippers. He carries a cane, but walks across the sidewalk quickly and energetically.

Pagoda waits for him at the top of the steps. They shake hands. Silence.

ROYAL

OK.

Pagoda opens the front door.

INT. LIVING ROOM. EVENING

Royal sits on a stool across from Richie and Margot on the couch. Chas stands at a table in the corner reading Richie's Atlas of the World. *Royal looks to Chas. Chas looks back at him but does not move. Royal looks back to Richie and Margot.*

ROYAL

I've missed the hell out of you, my darlings. You know that, don't you?

MARGOT

I hear you're dying.

ROYAL

So they tell me.

MARGOT

I'm sorry.

ROYAL
(*shrugs*)

I had a good run.

RICHIE

You don't look so sick, Dad.

ROYAL

Thank you.

RICHIE

What've you got?

ROYAL

I've got a pretty bad case of cancer.

CHAS
(*yawning*)
How long are you going to last?

Royal looks across the room at Chas. Chas does not look up from his atlas.

ROYAL

Not long.

CHAS

A month? A year?

ROYAL

About six weeks.

Royal looks back to Richie and Margot.

ROYAL

But let me get to the point. The three of you and your mother are all I've got, and I love you more than anything.

Chas laughs quietly.

ROYAL

Let me finish, Chas. Now, I've got six weeks to set things right with you, and I aim to do it. Will you give me a chance?

CHAS

No.

ROYAL

Do you speak for everyone?

CHAS

I speak for myself.

ROYAL

Well, you've made your views known. So why don't you let somebody else do some of the talking now?

MARGOT

What do you propose to do?

ROYAL

Well, I can't say, really. Make up for lost time, I suppose.
But the first thing I'd like to do is take you to see your
grandmother, at some point.

RICHIE
(*pause*)

I haven't been out there since I was six.

MARGOT

I haven't been there at all. I was never invited.

ROYAL

Well, she wasn't your real grandmother, so I didn't know
you'd be interested, sweetie. Anyway, you're invited this
time.

MARGOT

Thanks.

Richie looks to Chas. He looks back to Royal.

RICHIE

You know, Rachael's buried there, too.

ROYAL
(*pause*)

Who?

CHAS

My wife.

ROYAL

Oh. That's right, isn't it? Well, we can swing by her grave,
too.

*Chas slams the atlas shut and puts it back into the bookcase. He
walks toward the door. Royal extends his hand as Chas walks by.
Chas slaps it away and goes out of the room. Royal says to Margot
and Richie:*

ROYAL

I'll be right back.

INT. STAIRWAY. EVENING

Chas is already halfway to the second floor as Royal appears at the bottom of the steps.

ROYAL

Chas?

Chas stops. He looks down to Royal.

ROYAL

May I see my grandsons?

CHAS

Why?

ROYAL

Because I'd like to finally meet them.

Chas scoffs and shakes his head.

ROYAL

Don't give me that guff.

CHAS

I think we'll pass.

Chas walks away up the stairs. There is a clean square and a hook on the wall in the stairwell, as if something has been removed. Royal frowns. He yells toward the kitchen:

ROYAL

Pagoda! Where's my javelina?

INT. LIVING ROOM. NIGHT

Royal stands in the living room with Richie and Margot.

ROYAL

I'll say goodnight to you now, children.

Margot waves. Richie hugs Royal. Royal looks to be on the verge of tears.

ROYAL

Thank you, my sweet boy.

EXT. TENENBAUM HOUSE. NIGHT

Royal and Pagoda stand outside at the top of the front steps. Royal says quickly:

ROYAL

I'll contact you in the next twelve hours and give you further instructions.

Pagoda nods. A taxi stops in front of the house. Royal's face darkens. Henry and Etheline get out of the taxi. They each carry a playbill for a play called That Rascal. *Royal clamps his hand on Pagoda's arm and lets out a slow whistle.*

ROYAL

Look at that old grizzly bear.

Royal licks his fingers and smoothes back his hair. He bounds down the steps.

ROYAL

Hello, Ethel! Good evening, sir. Hold the cab, please, driver.

Henry leaves the door to the taxi open.

ETHELINE

Royal, this is Henry Sherman.

ROYAL

Hey, man. Lay it on me.

Royal puts out his hand for Henry to give him five. Henry reluctantly slaps hands with Royal and says:

HENRY

How do you do?

ROYAL
(*shrugs*)

Ah, what can I say? I'm dying.

Henry looks uneasy.

ETHELINE

Don't pay any attention to that man, Henry.

ROYAL

I'm just kidding. Goodnight, all.

Royal gets into the taxi and closes the door.

EXT. STREET. DAY

Margot and Eli walk together down a street with trash everywhere and abandoned cars and broken windows.

ELI

Right there is where I used to go get jacked off.

Margot nods. She seems distracted.

ELI

You don't give a shit.

MARGOT

I'm listening. (*Points to a deli.*) Right there is where you used to go get jacked off.

ELI

That's right.

They walk in silence for a minute.

ELI

How's Richie?

MARGOT
(*pause*)

I don't know. I can't tell.

ELI

Yeah. Me, neither. He wrote me a letter. He says he's in love with you.

MARGOT
(*frowns*)

What are you talking about?

ELI
(*shrugs*)

That's what he said. I don't know how we're supposed to take it. Hang on.

They stop in front of a partially demolished building. Eli presses the buzzer to one of the apartments. A voice comes on the call box:

> VOICE

Hello?

> ELI

Sugar, it's Eli.

> VOICE

Hey, baby.

The door buzzes open. Margot says blankly:

> MARGOT

What are we doing, Eli?

> ELI

I just got to pick something up. Don't repeat that, by the way. About Richie. It was told in confidence.

Eli goes inside. Margot stands alone on the street. She looks up at the destroyed building.

EXT. ARCHAEOLOGICAL EXCAVATION. DAY

A large network of pits between two brownstone town houses. There are workers digging, surveying, sketching, and shaking dirt through metal hand-screens.

Three archaeologists crouch around Etheline while she compares a bit of soil on the end of a trowel with a colour chart in a handbook. She is dressed entirely in denim except for a scarf over her hair. She has on sunglasses and boots. The three archaeologists are all scruffy young men with beards.

> ETHELINE

Good. Now I'll just remove the loose soil and note the decomposition levels.

Etheline dusts off a partially unearthed skeleton. Henry appears in the background, climbing down a ladder on the far side of the pit. He wears a grey wool suit and tie. He picks up a pebble off the ground and looks at it. Etheline says to the three archaeologists:

ETHELINE

These were probably slaves. Before the arrival of the –

GRADUATE STUDENT

What are you doing?

A graduate student with a shovel is looking at Henry and frowning.
Etheline and the three archaeologists turn around and see them.

GRADUATE STUDENT

Please, put that artefact back where you found it, sir.

Henry looks embarrassed. He puts the pebble back on the ground.

CUT TO:

Etheline and Henry walking through a trench together.

HENRY

I'm sorry to interrupt your work.

ETHELINE

Don't be silly.

HENRY

I just wanted to apologize for the other day. When I proposed
to you.

ETHELINE

Why? I thought it was very sweet.

HENRY

Look. I know I'm not as accomplished as some of the men
you've been involved with. Franklin Benedict and General
Cartwright and your ex-husband and –

ETHELINE

That's ridiculous.

HENRY

But I feel I have just as much to offer as any of them. I know
I went about it backwards, but –

ETHELINE

Henry, I have no interest in Frank Benedict or Doug
Cartwright. I never did.

54

Henry falls into a pit and disappears from view. Etheline does not notice this and continues walking.

ETHELINE

And as far as Royal is concerned, he's the most –

Etheline stops. She looks around. She sees Henry climbing quickly up a ladder, out of the pit. He is covered with dirt and has a small twig in his hair. She rushes over to him.

ETHELINE

Are you all right?

Henry sighs. He brushes some dirt off his jacket.

HENRY

I'm fine. Anyway, let me know when you make up your mind.

Henry starts to walk away. Etheline grabs his sleeve.

ETHELINE

Wait a second, Henry.

Henry stops. He looks to Etheline. She takes his hand and kisses it. He looks surprised.

ETHELINE

I'm sorry. I'm very nervous.

Etheline pulls the twig out of Henry's hair.

HENRY

That's OK. Thank you. Why are you –

ETHELINE

To tell you the truth, I haven't slept with a man in eighteen years.

Silence. Henry nods. He puts his hand on Etheline's cheek.

INT. MARGOT'S BEDROOM. DAY

Margot lies in her bed behind a mosquito net watching a downhill skiing competition on her portable television. Etheline stands in the doorway and says calmly:

ETHELINE

I think I'm falling for Henry.

Margot looks to Etheline. She pulls open the mosquito net.

MARGOT

That's amazing.

ETHELINE

What do you think of him?

MARGOT
(*excited*)

I think he's gorgeous.

ETHELINE

I'll tell you a secret. He's asked me to marry him.

MARGOT
(*dreamily*)

I'm going to have a father.

ETHELINE
(*hesitates*)

Well, I haven't accepted yet. Besides, you already have a father, sweetheart.

Not really. Plus, now he's dying.

CUT TO:

The hallway outside Margot's room. Pagoda is poised in the dark, watching from the stairs.

EXT. 375TH STREET Y ROOFTOP. DAY

A rooftop park with a chain-link fence around it. There are several fighters lifting weights and jumping rope. Ari does chin-ups from a jungle gym. Uzi does sit-ups on a mat. Buckley lays on the cement beside them.

Someone whistles from behind the fence. Ari and Uzi look. It is Royal. He is inside a telephone booth with the door partly open, holding the receiver to his ear. He signals for Ari and Uzi to come over.

Ari frowns. He looks across the courtyard to Anwar, sitting on a bench, reading a B.M.W. owner's manual. Royal ducks back into the telephone booth and holds the receiver to his ear. Anwar does not look up.

Ari slides down a fire-station-type pole. He and Uzi cautiously go over to the fence with Buckley. Royal hangs up the receiver and comes out of the telephone booth.

ROYAL

That's a hell of an old hound dog you got there. What's he go by?

ARI

Buckley.

ROYAL
(*pointing at Buckley*)

Buckley. Sit.

Buckley sits. Royal looks impressed. He turns to Ari.

ROYAL

You know who I am?

Ari shakes his head.

57

ROYAL

I'm Royal. You heard of me?

Ari nods. Royal looks pleased. His expression becomes serious again.

ROYAL

I'm very sorry for your loss. Your mother was a terribly
attractive woman.

ARI
(*pause*)

Thank you.

ROYAL

Which one are you?

ARI

Ari.

ROYAL
(*looks to Uzi*)

Uzi, I'm your granddad.

UZI

Hello.

ROYAL

I'm sorry we haven't gotten to know each other. I don't get
invited around much. What do you think about that, by the
way? You don't have to say anything.

Royal sighs. He stares off into space.

ROYAL

Kind of a fuck-you to the old man, I guess.

Royal looks back to Ari and Uzi.

ROYAL

How's your daddy?

ARI

Fine.

ROYAL

You think so? How often's he got you working out?

ARI

Sixteen times a week.

ROYAL
(*shakes his head*)
Do me a favour. Tell him you want to meet me.

UZI

But we just met.

ROYAL

No, we didn't.

Ari and Uzi look confused.

ROYAL

Look. I want us to have a relationship, but we're going to have to pull some strings to make it happen. (*Pause.*) Here's what you tell him . . .

INT. CHAS' BEDROOM. DAY

Ari and Uzi sit across from Chas. He is behind his desk with his back turned to them. Ari and Uzi are both dressed in black Adidas warm-ups. Chas wears his red one. A technician tinkers with a large Xerox machine on the other side of the room. Another technician rolls in a crate on a dolly.

ARI

I bet Mom would've wanted us to meet him before he died, wouldn't she?

Chas turns his chair around and looks to Ari and Uzi. Silence. He sighs.

EXT. CEMETERY. DAY

A small cemetery next to an electrical power plant. The trees are bare, and the city is across the river. Chas, Ari and Uzi stand together dressed in black Adidas warm-ups. Royal and Richie stand beside them.

Royal's mother's gravestone reads Helen O'Reilly Tenenbaum (1909–1962). Epitaph: The Salt of the Earth. Royal places a bouquet of white flowers at the foot of the grave. There are tears in his eyes. He says to Chas:

ROYAL

She was a tough old broad, wasn't she?

CHAS

I wouldn't know. Excuse me.

ROYAL

Oh, that's right. We got another body buried out here.
Hang on. Take some of these.

*Royal takes half of the flowers off his mother's grave and hands them
to Chas. Chas walks away. Silence.*

ROYAL

What do you think of this big old black buck moving in up
there?

RICHIE
(*pause*)

Who?

ROYAL

Henry Sherman. You know him?

RICHIE

Yeah.

ROYAL

Is he worth a damn?

I believe so.

Royal nods.

CUT TO:

Ari, Uzi and Margot standing in front of Rachael's gravestone, which reads Rachael Evans Tenenbaum (1965–2000). Uzi stares at Margot's missing finger.

UZI

What happened to your finger?

Ari looks quickly to Uzi.

MARGOT

It got chopped off by an axe.

UZI

How'd it get chopped off by –

ARI

Uzi. Shh.

MARGOT

It's OK. I'll tell you. I'm adopted. Did you know that?

Uzi shakes his head.

MARGOT

Well, I am. And I went to find my real family when I was fourteen. They live in Indiana.

EXT. FARM. DAY

A fourteen-year-old Margot stands behind a barn with a family of blond farmers. There are a mother and father and five very young children. Margot's hair is dyed black, and she wears a black Lacoste dress, black eyeliner, and black nail polish.

FATHER

Now just set one of them hickory trunks right up top there, sister Maggie.

Margot sets a log sideways on top of a wood pile. She reaches to adjust the log slightly just as the father swings an axe and chops the log in half.

Everyone looks stunned. The father stares at Margot's bloody hand. Margot looks to the father as if he is an idiot.

CUT TO:

Margot, Ari and Uzi standing together.

ARI
Did you try to sew it back on?

MARGOT
(*shakes her head*)
Couldn't find it.

CUT TO:

Richie and Royal looking at an impressive monument in the middle of the cemetery. An inscription says: Veteran of Two Wars. Father of Nine Children. Drowned in the Caspian Sea.

ROYAL
That's a hell of a damn grave.

Richie nods. Royal says wistfully:

ROYAL
I wish it were mine.

CUT TO:

Royal and Richie walking together among the gravestones.

ROYAL
It's a shame, isn't it?

RICHIE
What?

ROYAL
You probably had another good two to three years of competitive play in you.

RICHIE
(*shrugs*)

Probably.

ROYAL

I had a lot riding on that match, you know. Financially and personally.

Richie nods. Silence.

ROYAL

Why'd you choke out there that day, Baumer?

RICHIE
(*pause*)

I don't know, Dad.

INSERT:

A television set tuned in to network coverage of a tennis match on grass courts. Richie is playing an Indian player dressed all in white. A title identifies him as Sanjay Gandhi.

Gandhi serves. With a bizarre swing, Richie hits his return directly off the court and deep into the stands. He shakes his head and talks to himself. It is briefly revealed that he is wearing no shoes and only one sock.

ANNOUNCER
(*voice over*)

That's seventy-two unforced errors for Richie Tenenbaum. He's playing the worst tennis of his life. What's he feeling right now, Tex Hayward?

TEX HAYWARD
(*voice over*)

I don't know, Jim. There's obviously something wrong with him. He's taken off his shoes and one of his socks, and – actually, I think he's crying.

Richie is shown preparing to serve with tears all over his face. He hesitates. He looks into the stands.

ANNOUNCER
(*voice over*)
Who's he looking at in the friends' box, Tex?

Margot and Raleigh, holding hands, watch from their seats in a courtside box. They look very concerned.

TEX HAYWARD
(*voice over*)
That's his sister, Margot, and her new husband, Raleigh St. Clair. They were just married yesterday, Jim.

Richie stares at Margot and Raleigh. He looks to Chas, with Rachael, Ari and Uzi. He looks to Etheline. He looks to Royal in a lonely seat up in the nosebleed section. Royal stands up and walks towards the exit.

Richie serves suddenly, underhand, barely tossing the ball into the air. Gandhi nails his return, and Richie attempts to play it by throwing his racquet at the ball.

CUT TO:

Royal and Richie standing together.

ROYAL
I kind of disappeared after that, didn't I?

RICHIE
(*shrugs*)
Yeah, but I understood. I know you're not very good with disappointment.

Royal nods. He kicks a pebble on the ground.

CUT TO:

Royal scraping some dirt off Rachael's gravestone with his foot. Chas stands beside him.

ROYAL
You still got that little B.B. in your hand, Chassie?

Chas looks to Royal. He holds up his hand and shows Royal a little round bump in between two knuckles. Royal taps it with his finger. It moves slightly.

CHAS

Why'd you shoot me?

Silence. Royal says quietly:

ROYAL

It was the object of the game, wasn't it?

CHAS

No. We were on the same team.

ROYAL

(*pause*)

Were we?

Chas does not respond. Royal sighs.

ROYAL

Well, you sued me. Twice. And got me disbarred. But I don't hold it against you, do I?

INT. JUDGE'S CHAMBERS. DAY

A lawyer in a robe sits behind his desk. Chas and Royal and two attorneys sit across from him. A stenographer sits at a metal stand, typing.

JUDGE

And how was it possible for Mr Tenenbaum to withdraw these funds without your written authorization?

ROYAL

Objection, your honour. Now, dammit –

ROYAL'S LAWYER

This isn't a courtroom, Royal. Don't object.

CHAS

Because I started the corporation when I was a minor, so my father was the primary signatory on most of my accounts.

Chas' attorney whispers something in he ear.

CHAS

He also stole bonds out of my safety deposit box when I was fourteen.

The judge looks to Royal. Royal looks guilty.

CUT TO:

Royal and Chas standing with Ari and Uzi.

ROYAL

You think you could start forgiving me?

CHAS

Why should I?

ROYAL

Because you're hurting me.

Chas turns and walks away. Uzi looks to Royal.

UZI

Were you in prison?

ROYAL

Kind of. Minimum security. I got jacked by the I.R.S. Should we split?

ARI

Yes, sir.

ROYAL

Call me Mr Tenenbaum.

ARI

OK.

ROYAL

I'm kidding. Call me Pappy.

ARI

OK.

Royal yells across the cemetery to Richie and Margot:

ROYAL

Come on! Let's shag ass!

CUT TO:

Margot and Richie walking toward the cemetery gates.

RICHIE

How are you and Raleigh getting along? You think you're going to get back together?

MARGOT
(*pause*)

I don't know.

RICHIE
(*shrugs*)

Well, if you need someone to talk to, let me know, OK? I like Raleigh very much. I know he's a lot older than you are, and you're having some problems, but – Anyway, maybe I can help.

MARGOT

OK. Thanks.

A maintenance man with a shovel in his hand yells from across the cemetery:

MAINTENANCE MAN

Hey, Baumer! All right!

Richie smiles and waves to the maintenance man.

MARGOT

By the way, I heard about that letter you sent to Eli.

Silence. Richie starts to say something. He hesitates. A pack of cigarettes falls out of Margot's pocket on to the ground. They stop walking and look at it.

RICHIE

You dropped some cigarettes.

MARGOT

Those aren't mine.

RICHIE

Well, they just fell out of your pocket.

Margot picks up the pack of cigarettes and puts it back in her pocket.

INT. ELI CASH'S TOWN HOUSE. DAY

Eli walks into the vestibule smoking a joint which he keeps in his mouth at all times like a cigarette. He opens the front door. Richie stands on the top step.

ELI

Oh, my Lord. Look at you.

Eli embraces Richie. They smile sadly at each other.

CUT TO:

Richie and Eli walking into the front room of the house. It is furnished like a house in the English countryside, with antiques and potted flowers and old rugs.

RICHIE

Did you tell Margot about that letter I wrote to you?

ELI
(*hesitates*)

Why? Did she mention it?

Richie does not respond.

ELI

Yes, I did.

RICHIE

Eli, that was meant to be just between you and me.

ELI

I know. I'm sorry. Why would she have repeated that, I wonder?

RICHIE

Well, I would ask you the same question.

ELI
(*pause*)

Rightly so.

INT. STUDIO. DAY

Richie and Eli walk into the next room. Eli's wife, Sabrina, is painting in her studio. She is very beautiful and wears spectacles and a white sari. She is barefoot. Classical music plays quietly on the record player.

ELI

Sabrina?

Sabrina does not look up. She seems irritated.

SABRINA

What?

ELI

Look what I found on the doorstep.

Sabrina looks to Richie. She is only mildly surprised. She has an English accent.

SABRINA

Hello, darling.

Sabrina hugs and kisses Richie.

ELI

Charlotte? Stetson? Say hello to Uncle Richie.

There are two children in the corner. Stetson is six. He works at a spinning potter's wheel, moulding a hunk of clay. Charlotte is five. She is painting a set of teacups. She has a cast in a sling on her arm. They are both blond and fair.

The children do not respond to Eli. Eli does not appear to notice this, as he is in the process of relighting his joint.

RICHIE

How'd she break her arm?

ELI
(sadly)
I fell down the stairs with her.

Richie looks disturbed. He notices a nude, teenaged girl standing on the table. She has a deep tan, except where she wore a bikini. She is Sabrina's model, Cinnamon.

69

ELI

That's Cinnamon. Hello, Cinnamon.

Cinnamon looks at Eli coldly.

INT. ELI'S STUDY. DAY

Eli sits on a couch across from Richie. They are both drinking wine. There is a large zip-lock bag of marijuana on the table. There is a large, frightening painting on the wall of five men wearing African masks and sitting on dirt-bikes.

Silence.

ELI

What'd you say?

RICHIE
(*pause*)

Hm?

ELI

What?

RICHIE

I didn't say anything.

ELI

When? Right now? (*Pause.*) I'm sorry. Don't listen to me. (*barely audible*) I'm on mescaline. I've been spaced out all day.

Eli pours himself another glass of wine.

RICHIE

Did you say you're on mescaline?

ELI
(*nods*)

I did, indeed. Very much so.

Richie reflects on this for a minute.

RICHIE

How often do you –

ELI

I'm worried about you, Richie.

RICHIE
(*pause*)

Why?

ELI

Well, actually, Margot is, for some reason. But I did find it odd when you said you were in love with her. (*Pause.*) She's married, you know.

RICHIE

Yeah.

ELI

And she's your sister.

RICHIE
(*quickly*)

Adopted.

INSERT:

Page 112 of The Royal Tenenbaums. *It says Chapter Five.*

EXT. LINDBERGH PALACE HOTEL. DAY

The side entrance of the hotel. Royal goes in through the revolving doors.

INT. LOBBY. DAY

Royal comes into the lobby and freezes.

A large number of trunks, suitcases and boxes are stacked and piled on four carts next to the front desk. There are also several dozen hanging garments on a rack with wheels on it. A bellboy rolls a fifth cart next to the others. The manager and his assistant come over and watch Royal study his possessions. Royal says suddenly:

ROYAL

Where're my encyclopedias?

MANAGER

They've been placed in storage.

ROYAL
(*shaking his head*)

Damn you. You're taking my encyclopedias. This is
humiliating.

MANAGER

I'm sorry. Would you like to –

ROYAL

Where am I supposed to go? You're turning me into a
goddamn hobo.

MANAGER

I'd be happy to make a reservation for you at another hotel.

ROYAL

You son of a bitch.

MANAGER

Frederick?

*The manager looks to the bellboy. The bellboy begins to roll one of the
carts across the lobby. The manager walks away. Dusty, the elevator
operator, appears at Royal's side.*

ROYAL

Hello, Dusty.

DUSTY

Hello, sir.

ROYAL

Spot me a quarter, will you?

DUSTY

Of course.

INT. TELEPHONE BOOTH. DAY

Royal places a call from the lobby.

ROYAL

Richie? It's your dad.

INT. DINING ROOM. NIGHT

Etheline, Henry, Chas, Margot, Richie, Ari and Uzi sit at the table eating dessert.

RICHIE

I think he's very lonely. Lonelier than he lets on, and maybe lonelier than he even realizes.

ETHELINE

Have you spoken to him about this?

RICHIE

Briefly. And he agreed that –

CHAS

I'm sorry. Maybe I'm a little confused. What are you suggesting?

RICHIE

That he come here and stay in my room.

CHAS

Are you out of your mind?

RICHIE
(*sincerely*)
No, I'm not. Anyway, I think he'd be much more comfortable here than –

CHAS

Who gives a shit?

RICHIE

I do.

CHAS

You poor sucker. You poor, washed-up poppa's boy.

Henry puts his hand gently on Chas' arm.

HENRY

All right. Let's not get out of hand.

Chas jerks his arm away.

CHAS

Don't get in the middle of this, Mr Sherman. This is a family matter.

MARGOT

Don't talk to him like that.

HENRY

Please, call me Henry.

CHAS

I prefer Mr Sherman.

ETHELINE

Call him Henry.

CHAS

Why? I don't know him that well.

ETHELINE

You've known him for ten years.

CHAS

As your accountant, Mr Sherman, yes.

ARI
(*to Richie*)

Where are you going to sleep?

RICHIE

I'll just camp out upstairs.

UZI

We brought an extra sleeping bag you can use.

RICHIE

Oh, that's OK. I've got an old Scout cot and a couple of army blankets.

UZI

You want to borrow our electric –

CHAS

Uzi.

ARI

We don't mind, Dad. We like him.

UZI

Who? Pappy?

Chas looks shocked and then revolted.

CHAS

It's not your decision, goddammit.

ETHELINE

Nor is it yours.

RICHIE

Well, he's already up there.

Silence.

RICHIE

I think he's asleep, because of the medication he's on. But I guess you can wake him up and throw him out, if Mom says it's OK.

INT. RICHIE'S BEDROOM. NIGHT

Richie's room has been converted into a makeshift hospital room. Royal lies on an electric hospital bed. He has an I.V. in his arm and a tube in his nose. There are several monitors and machines breathing and humming. There are numerous bottles of pills and medicines on the nightstand. Pagoda has on a surgical mask and scrubs.

Chas stands in the doorway. Richie is behind him.

CHAS

Get out.

ROYAL

All right. Let me just collect my things.

Royal sits up on the edge of the bed. He is dressed in pink surgical scrubs.

ROYAL

Would you mind handing me my cane, Richie?

Richie hands Royal his cane. Royal struggles to his feet. He rolls the I.V. stand beside him.

ROYAL

Let's see, now. Where's my suitcase?

Royal's knee gives out. He staggers a step. He grips the back of a chair and looks to Richie with a surprised expression. He collapses on to the floor. He produces a wooden spoon, which he takes between his teeth.

RICHIE

Dad?

Richie and Pagoda rush over and kneel on the floor beside Royal. Chas frowns. Richie yells out the door:

RICHIE

Mom!

ROYAL

Grab me a Nembutal, son.

Richie runs to the night stand and pops open a bottle of pills. Chas looks down at Royal.

CHAS

Are you OK?

Royal takes the spoon out of his mouth.

ROYAL

Fuck do you care?

Richie gives Royal a pill with a glass of water. Etheline comes to the door.

ETHELINE

Oh, my goodness!

ROYAL

Pagoda. Call Dr McClure.

CUT TO:

Forty-five minutes later. Royal is back in bed. He is being examined by Dusty, the elevator operator from the Lindbergh Palace. Dusty is

76

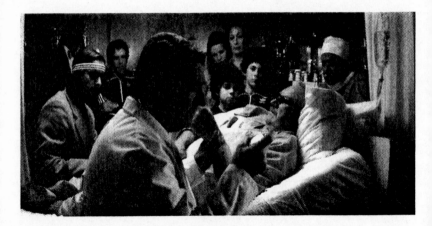

dressed in a white lab coat and elevator-operator pants with a red stripe down the side. He checks Royal's pulse while everyone watches.

INT. HALLWAY. NIGHT

Dusty speaks with the Tenenbaums in the hallway outside Richie's bedroom.

> DUSTY
> His condition is stable. The attack was just a side effect. I recommend that you push fluids and continue the stomach cancer medication.

Dusty's beeper goes off. He looks at it.

INSERT:

Dusty's beeper. It has a digital message on it:

> Smitty worked a double yesterday. Can you sub for him tonight?

CUT TO:

Dusty pushing a button on his beeper.

> CHAS
> Can we move him?

DUSTY

Absolutely not.

CHAS

For how long?

DUSTY

We'll have to wait and see.

RICHIE

Is he going to be all right?

DUSTY

That depends. Is he a fighter?

RICHIE

Yeah.

DUSTY
(*solemnly*)

Then that's the best we've got. Now, if you'll excuse me, I have another call to make.

INT. RICHIE'S BEDROOM. NIGHT

Etheline sits next to Royal's bed. Pagoda comes in and hands Royal a small brown paper sack.

ROYAL

Pagoda is in possession of a parcel that contains my will and some instructions regarding the funeral, including my epitaph, for when the time comes.

Etheline nods.

ROYAL

Proof-read it for me before they carve it on the headstone, OK?

ETHELINE

OK.

ROYAL

I never did stop loving you, by the way. Do you believe that?

ETHELINE

Not really.

ROYAL

You look terrific. That dress is stunning.

ETHELINE
(*pause*)

Thanks.

Royal raises an eyebrow. Etheline shakes her head and goes out of the room. Royal opens the paper sack and withdraws a cheeseburger wrapped in aluminium foil. He unwraps it and takes a bite. He hesitates. Henry is standing in the doorway. He walks away.

A dalmatian mouse eats some crumbs off the floor.

CUT TO:

An hour later. Royal lies in bed, drinking a milkshake, reading a spy novel. Chas appears in the doorway.

CHAS

Lights out, old man.

Chas turns out the light.

ROYAL

I was going to read for a little bit, Chas.

CHAS

Sorry. 11.30. Lights out.

ROYAL

I'm in the middle of a sentence.

CHAS

Have to finish it up in the morning. Them's the rules.

Silence. Royal says in a quiet, strangely upbeat voice in the darkness:

ROYAL

Goodnight, m'boy.

Chas hesitates. He closes the door.

INT. BALLROOM. NIGHT

The ballroom on the top floor of the house. There are chairs and tables with sheets over them lined up along the walls. Near the centre of the room, there is a yellow nylon pup-tent. The room is dark except for a lamp glowing inside the tent.

INT. TENT. NIGHT

There is a Boy Scout sleeping bag on an air mattress on a cot inside the tent. There is a photograph of the Tenenbaum family taped to the nylon wall. There is a small table with a stack of books and some of Richie's Matchbox cars and tennis trophies on it. Richie lies on the cot reading Three Plays by Margot Tenenbaum.

Chas comes into the tent. Richie looks up, startled.

> CHAS
>
> Looks like you and Dad are back together again, huh?

> RICHIE
>
> *(pause)*
>
> He's your dad, too, Chas.

> CHAS
>
> No, he's not. (*Pause.*) You really hate me, don't you?

> RICHIE
>
> *(puzzled)*
>
> No, I don't. I love you.

Chas looks disturbed by this.

> CHAS
>
> Well, I don't know what you think you're going to get out of this. But believe me, whatever it is, it's not worth it.

> RICHIE
>
> I don't want to hurt you, Chas. I know what you and the boys have been through. You're my brother, and I love you.

> CHAS
>
> *(gritting his teeth)*
>
> Stop saying that.

EXT. RICHIE'S BEDROOM. DAY

The next morning. Royal sits on the window sill smoking a cigarette. Pagoda sits next to him drinking a cup of coffee. Royal throws his cigarette out the window. He looks down at the street. He frowns.

Eli is climbing out a window on the second floor.

ROYAL

What's that jackass doing here?

Pagoda looks down at Eli. Eli drops to the sidewalk. He sees Royal's cigarette burning on the ground. He steps on it. He looks up to Royal. Their eyes meet. Royal yells:

ROYAL

I know you, asshole!

Eli hesitates. He smiles defiantly. He runs away.

INSERT:

An article on Eli in the Sunday magazine section. The headline says Where the Wild Things Are. There is a photograph of Eli in the desert holding a dead rattlesnake by the tail in each hand. A note stapled to the top says:

Dear Mrs Tenenbaum, Just in case you missed it. Love, Eli.

CUT TO:

Margot and Etheline sitting together in Etheline's study. Margot is reading Henry's book, Accounting for Everything. *Etheline is reading the article on Eli. Margot looks at it.*

MARGOT

Did Eli send you that?

ETHELINE
(*nods*)
He always sends me his clippings.

MARGOT
(*incredulous*)

What for?

ETHELINE

I think he just likes the encouragement. He's done it for
years. He used to send me his grades in college.

MARGOT
(*frowns*)

That's ridiculous.

*There is a rap on the glass. Margot and Etheline look up. Raleigh is
standing in the window. He looks miserable.*

EXT. GARDEN. DAY

The backyard. Margot and Raleigh sit at a metal table drinking tea.

RALEIGH

How long do you intend to stay here?

MARGOT

I don't know.

RALEIGH

Are you ever coming home?

MARGOT
(*pause*)

Maybe not. But –

RALEIGH

You're joking.

MARGOT

No. But –

RALEIGH

I want to die.

*Raleigh crumples into a ball on the ground and stays there. Margot
puts her hand on his back.*

MARGOT

Raleigh, please. For God's sake.

Raleigh sits up suddenly.

RALEIGH

Have you met someone else?

MARGOT
(*pause*)
I couldn't begin to even think about knowing how to
answer that question.

Raleigh stands up and walks away.

INT. HALLWAY. DAY

*Royal watches down the stairwell as Margot comes up. He knocks on
the railing. She looks up at him. Silence.*

ROYAL
I don't like the way you're treating Raleigh.

MARGOT
What are you talking about? You don't even know him.

ROYAL
I've met him. And I don't think he deserves –

MARGOT
Stay out of it.

*Margot walks toward her room. Royal steps on to the landing at the
top of the stairs.*

ROYAL
You're two-timing him with that bloodsucker Eli Cash.

Margot stops. She stands still with her back to Royal.

ROYAL
It's not right, dammit. You used to be a genius.

*Margot turns to Royal. They look at each other for a long minute.
She says in a quiet voice:*

MARGOT
No, I didn't.

ROYAL
(*hesitates*)
Well, anyway, that's what they used to say.

Margot goes into her room and closes the door.

EXT. ROOF. DAY

Raleigh stands at the edge of the roof looking down to the ground while Richie cleans the empty falcon's coop.

> RALEIGH
>
> Richard, I know you're terribly close to Margot, and perhaps you understand her better than anyone.

> RICHIE
>
> I doubt it.

> RALEIGH
>
> Nevertheless, may I confide in you?

> RICHIE
> (*pause*)
>
> OK.

> RALEIGH
>
> I believe she's having an affair.

Silence. Richie comes out of the coop and goes over to Raleigh.

> RALEIGH
>
> I'm utterly devastated. I don't know where else to turn. Will you advise me?

> RICHIE
>
> I don't know. What do you want to do?

RALEIGH

Well, I thought, perhaps –

RICHIE

Find the guy and get him?

RALEIGH
(*pause*)
Well, no. I thought we might –

Richie punches his hand through the attic window. He kicks it. Raleigh looks shocked. He stares at Richie's bloody hand.

RICHIE

Who do you think it might be?

RALEIGH
(*hesitates*)
I don't know, at the moment.

INT. CHAS' BEDROOM. DAY

Royal comes down the hallway and looks in the doorway to Chas' room. There are five computers, four telephones, the Xerox machine and a television and V.C.R. on a cart. Three secretaries make copies and take messages. Chas is on the telephone. A messenger waits for him to sign a document.

Ari and Uzi sit working with a calculator and a ledger pad at a small desk in the corner. Royal says to them:

ROYAL

Let's go down to Little Tokyo and get some firecrackers.

Chas covers the receiver with his hand.

CHAS

What do you need?

ROYAL
(*hesitates*)
Nothing. You got them crunching numbers for you, huh?

CHAS

Please, don't come in this room.

INT. ETHELINE'S STUDY. DAY

Etheline sits at her desk writing numbers on little bits of pottery and recording it in a notebook. Royal stands in the garden, looking in the window. His I.V. bag hangs on a rolling stand beside him.

> ROYAL
>
> Chassie's got those boys cooped up like a pair of jack-rabbits, Ethel.

> ETHELINE
>
> He has his reasons.

> ROYAL
>
> I know it. But you can't raise boys to be scared of life. You got to brew some recklessness into them.

> ETHELINE
>
> I think that's terrible advice.

> ROYAL
> (*pause*)
>
> No, you don't.

INT. RICHIE'S BEDROOM. DAY

Royal listens to Ari over the intercom while Pagoda does yoga exercises in the corner:

> ARI
> (*voice over*)
>
> We take boxing and self-defence class.

Royal pushes a button to talk.

> ROYAL
>
> I'm not talking about dance lessons. I'm talking about putting a brick through the other guy's windshield. I'm talking about taking it out and chopping it up.

Silence. Ari says over the intercom:

> ARI
> (*voice over*)
>
> What do you mean?

MONTAGE:

(Royal, Ari and Uzi laugh continuously throughout the following montage.)

Royal, Ari and Uzi jump off a high scaffold into the indoor pool at the 375th Street Y.

Royal, Ari and Uzi jaywalk through heavy traffic.

Royal, Ari and Uzi ride horses in the park. Royal leads them at a full gallop down a ravine and over a stone wall.

Royal, Ari and Uzi race go-carts up and down loading ramps and in between fork-lifts in a large warehouse.

Royal, Ari and Uzi throw water balloons at a gypsy cab.

Royal, Ari and Uzi hide cartons of chocolate milk under their jackets and walk quickly out the door of a bodega.

Royal, Ari and Uzi ride on the back of a speeding garbage truck.

EXT. STREET. DAY

Royal, Ari, Uzi and Pagoda are at the dogfights. Pagoda throws a fifty-dollar bill into a pile of money on the sidewalk. Ari and Uzi each throw in a dollar. Royal motions to Pagoda.

> ROYAL
> He saved my life, you know. Thirty years ago. I was knifed at a bazaar in Calcutta, and he carried me to the hospital on his back.

> ARI
> Who stabbed you?

Royal motions to Pagoda again.

> ROYAL
> He did. There was a price on my head, and he was a hired assassin. Stuck me in the gut with a shiv.

INT. CHAS' BEDROOM. DAY

The three secretaries are still at work, and Chas is on the telephone. He sees Royal, Ari and Uzi walking by in the hallway. Chas hangs up the telephone.

> CHAS
> Where've you been?

Chas goes to the doorway. He glares at Ari, Uzi and Royal.

> ROYAL
> Just stepped out to get some air. How's the –

88

CHAS
(*concerned*)

What's that?

Chas points to a spot of dried blood on Uzi's forehead.

ROYAL

Holy shit. That's not – What is that?

Royal licks his finger and rubs away the blood.

ROYAL

No. That's dog's blood.

Chas frowns. He looks to Royal. Royal hesitates. Chas grabs Royal by the arm and pulls him into the closet across the hall.

INT. CLOSET. DAY

Chas closes the door and turns on the light. There are hundreds of board games, most of which are about thirty years old, in shelves up to the ceiling.

CHAS

Stay away from my children. Do you understand?

ROYAL
(*looking around*)

My God. I haven't been in here in years.

CHAS
(*screams*)

Are you listening to me?

ROYAL

Yes, I am. And I think you're having a nervous breakdown. I don't believe you've recovered from Rachael's death. I think –

Chas turns off the light, goes out of the closet, and closes the door. Royal stands alone in the dark. He switches the light back on and looks down at the floor. He smiles.

ROYAL

There you are.

The stuffed boar's head is under the bottom shelf, in the corner, covered with dust.

EXT. PARK. DAY

Royal and Etheline walk along a path through the park. Royal rolls his hanging I.V. bag at his side.

> ETHELINE
>
> How are you feeling?

> ROYAL
>
> Oh, I'm having a ball. Scrapping and yelling. Mixing it up. Loving every minute with this damn crew. (*sincerely*) I'd like to thank you for raising our children, by the way.

> ETHELINE
> (*pause*)
>
> OK.

> ROYAL
>
> I'm not kidding.

Etheline shrugs.

> ROYAL
>
> You always put them first, didn't you?

> ETHELINE
>
> I tried to. Lately, I feel like maybe I didn't do such a great job.

> ROYAL
>
> Goddammit, don't do that to yourself. I'm the one that failed them. Or, anyway, it's nobody's fault. (*Pause.*) Plus, it doesn't –

> ETHELINE
>
> Well, then why didn't you give a damn about us, Royal? Why didn't you care?

> ROYAL
>
> I don't know, but I'm ashamed of myself. I'll tell you one thing, though. You've got more grit, and fire, and guts than any bob-tailed fox I ever damn hunted, and if –

Etheline laughs. Royal smiles.

> ROYAL

What? What's so funny?

> ETHELINE

Nothing.

> ROYAL

No, tell me.

> ETHELINE

Nothing. Just these little expressions of yours.

> ROYAL
> *(pause)*

I don't know what you're talking about. But I'll take it as a compliment.

They look at each other for a long minute.

> ROYAL

You're true blue, Ethel. You really are.

CUT TO:

Henry with two bags of groceries in his arms, watching from behind a stone wall above the path. He listens as Royal says:

> ROYAL

How's your love life?

> ETHELINE

None of your business.

Henry frowns.

INSERT:

Page 147 of The Royal Tenenbaums. *It says Chapter Six.*

EXT. SIDEWALK. EVENING

Etheline and Henry come down the front steps of the Tenenbaum house. Henry is dressed in black tie. The ends of a pair of theatre tickets stick out of his breast pocket. Pagoda holds a gypsy cab for them at the curb.

HENRY

I'd like you to talk to Royal about us, if you don't mind.

ETHELINE
(*hesitates*)

I don't think the timing's right for that, Henry.

HENRY

Well, I'd agree if I thought he was really going to die in six weeks. But I don't.

Etheline stops at the bottom of the steps. Silence.

ETHELINE

Well, I hope you're right. (*Pause.*) Actually, I don't believe I'm going to join you tonight. I'll call you in the morning.

Etheline turns around and goes back up the steps. Henry watches her. He looks sad and stunned. Pagoda watches Henry. Etheline goes inside and closes the door.

INT. CLOSET. NIGHT

Royal and Pagoda stand together in the board-game-filled closet drinking Martinis and smoking cigarettes. Royal has a half-eaten cheeseburger in his hand. He whispers excitedly:

ROYAL

She said that?

Pagoda nods. Royal snaps his fingers.

ROYAL

We got the sucker on the ropes.

INT. KITCHEN. DAY

The next morning. Henry stands at the counter reading the Wall Street Journal. *He has on reading glasses. Royal comes into the kitchen eating a cheeseburger. Henry looks at him blankly. Royal sits on a stool.*

92

ROYAL

Can I ask you something, Hank?

HENRY
(*pause*)

OK.

ROYAL

Are you trying to steal my woman?

HENRY
(*pause*)

I beg your pardon?

ROYAL

You heard me, Coltrane.

HENRY
(*long pause*)

Coltrane?

ROYAL

What?

HENRY

Did you just call me Coltrane?

ROYAL

No.

HENRY

You didn't?

ROYAL

No.

HENRY
(*pause*)

OK.

ROYAL

But if I did?

Silence. Henry waits for Royal to continue.

ROYAL

You wouldn't be able to do anything about it, would you?

HENRY

You don't think so?

ROYAL

No, I don't.

HENRY
(*seething*)
Listen, Royal. If you think –

ROYAL

You want to talk some jive?

Henry hesitates. He looks puzzled.

ROYAL

I'll talk some jive with you.

Royal stands up. He screams:

ROYAL

I'll talk some jive like you never heard!

HENRY
(*yelling*)

Oh, yeah?

ROYAL

Right on!

HENRY

Sit down!

ROYAL

What?

Royal starts doing a little dance in front of Henry.

ROYAL

What'd you say?

HENRY

I said, sit down, goddammit!

ROYAL

Oh, I heard you.

Henry jumps to his feet. Royal stops dancing. He says darkly:

> ROYAL
>
> I want you out of my house.

> HENRY
>
> This is not your house.

> ROYAL
>
> Don't play semantics with me. I want your raggedy ass back on the –

> ETHELINE
>
> What's going on here?

Henry and Royal look to Etheline. She stands in the doorway.

> ROYAL
>
> Nothing.

Royal goes to the refrigerator and opens it. He takes out a jar of peanut butter and a jar of grape jelly. Etheline looks to Henry. Henry walks out of the room.

INT. RICHIE'S BEDROOM. DAY

Henry goes into Richie's room and takes a bottle of Royal's pills off the night stand. He goes back out of the room.

INT. TELEPHONE ROOM. DAY

Henry reads the label on the bottle while he places a call.

> HENRY
>
> Hello. I'm calling in regards to a Dr McClure. Yes. At Colby General. The name of the patient is Royal Tenenbaum.

Henry takes out a pill and examines it.

INSERT:

The pill. It has pink and blue sparkles all over it and the word Tic-Tac printed on the side.

INT. STAIRWAY. DAY

Henry goes up the stairs with a cold, determined look on his face. He has the bottle of pills in his hand.

INT. PAGODA'S ROOM. DAY

A small room with an Indian pattern on the wallpaper. Pagoda lies on a hammock listening to Indian music on a portable record player. There is a knock on the door, and then it opens. Henry stands in the doorway. He stares at Pagoda.

                    HENRY
How much is he paying you?

Pagoda looks scared.

INSERT:

A television set tuned in to an interview show. The host is a tall, distinguished-looking man in his fifties. He is Peter Bradley. Eli is his guest. They sit at a round table lit at the centre of a pitch-black room.

                    ELI
Well, I grew up with the Tenenbaum family, you know.

                    PETER
Right. They've come on hard times now, haven't they?

Eli nods sadly.

CUT TO:

Richie's room. Margot and Royal are watching Eli on television.

                    ROYAL
Bullshit. Change it.

The door opens. Richie comes into the room. His hand is wrapped with bloody bandages. Margot looks concerned.

                    MARGOT
What'd you do to your hand?

                    RICHIE
Nothing.

Richie goes into the closet. Two dalmatian mice dart out across the floor. They run under the radiator. Royal frowns.

ROYAL

You think we could get somebody to come over here and kill some of these mice for us?

MARGOT

No. Those belong to Chas. Or, anyway, he invented them.

Richie drags a large trunk out of the closet.

ROYAL

Well, tell him to stick them in a fucking cage or something.

Henry and Pagoda come into the room. Henry goes over to the intercom and presses a button on it.

HENRY

Etheline? Would you mind coming up here for a minute, please?

Royal looks at Henry suspiciously.

ROYAL

What's cooking, Pops?

HENRY

You'll see.

ETHELINE
(*on the intercom*)

OK.

INSERT:

The television set. Eli's interview continues.

PETER

Now, your previous novel –

ELI

Wildcattin'.

PETER

Right. Not a success. Why?

Hm. Well, *Wildcattin'* was written in a kind of obsolete vernacular, much like the –

Eli freezes. He looks quickly across the room.

ELI

Holy shit.

PETER
(*looking around*)

What?

A look of sheer horror crosses Eli's face. He braces himself against the edge of the table. Peter looks concerned.

PETER

Are you all right?

ELI
(*concerned*)

Why is it so dense in here?

Peter hesitates. Eli removes his microphone, stands up, and walks off the set. Peter Bradley watches him go.

CUT TO:

Everyone watching in Richie's bedroom. They look stunned.

ROYAL

Son of a bitch. What the hell kind of way to act is that?

RICHIE
(*pause*)

He's on drugs.

MARGOT
(*worried*)

I'll be right back.

Margot goes to the telephone. Etheline and Chas come into the room. Chas is eating a sandwich. Ari, Uzi and Buckley follow them.

HENRY

Hold on a minute, please.

Henry steps in front of the television set and turns it off.

HENRY

Pagoda has something to say.

Everyone looks to Pagoda. Silence. Pagoda looks worried. He turns to Royal and points at him.

PAGODA

He has the cancer.

HENRY
(*angrily*)

No, he doesn't.

Royal sits up. Henry stares at Royal.

HENRY

I know what stomach cancer looks like. I've seen it. And you don't eat three cheeseburgers a day with french fries when you've got it. The pain is excruciating.

ROYAL

How would you know?

HENRY

My wife had it.

Silence. Royal pulls out his I.V. and the other tubes that are attached to him. He goes into the bathroom and closes the door. Henry turns to Etheline.

HENRY

Not only is there no Dr McClure at Colby General, there's no Colby General. It closed in 1974.

Chas crushes his sandwich in his hand.

PAGODA

Ah, shit, man.

ETHELINE

But why would he –

Chas slams his hand against the bathroom door as hard as he can. He sits down on the bed and picks up the phone. He places a call.

CHAS

Yes. Can you send a taxi to 111 Archer Avenue? Right away, please. Thank you.

Chas hangs up. Royal comes out of the bathroom. He is fully dressed in a suit, and he is zipping up a small leather bag. He picks up one of his bottles of pills off the night stand and leaves the rest. He looks to Pagoda.

ROYAL

I guess we're back on the street, pal.

Etheline looks to Pagoda. She frowns. Pagoda looks uneasy.

ETHELINE

Were you a part of this?

HENRY

Of course he was.

Etheline looks to Royal. Royal looks to Pagoda. He says regretfully:

ROYAL

Time to come clean. No more lies.

Pagoda stares at Royal bitterly. Richie points at the hospital bed and life-support machines.

RICHIE

How'd you get all these medical supplies?

ROYAL
(*pause*)

A guy at St Pete's owed me a favor. I did some malpractice work for him. I do have high blood pressure, though.

Royal swallows one of his pills. He turns and stands in front of everyone.

ROYAL

Look. I know I'm the bad guy on this one, but I just want to say that the last six days have been the best six days of, probably, my whole life.

A strange, sad expression crosses Royal's face.

NARRATOR

Immediately after making this statement, Royal realized that it was true.

Royal begins to gather his possessions.

INT. HALLWAY. DAY

Royal comes out of Richie's room with his suitcases. Etheline stands at the end of the hall.

ETHELINE

Why'd you do this to us, Royal?

Royal stops.

ETHELINE

What was the point?

ROYAL
(*pause*)

I thought maybe I could win you back. Or, anyway, I thought I could get rid of Henry and keep things status quo.

ETHELINE

But we hadn't spoken in seven years.

ROYAL

I know. Plus, I was broke, and I got kicked out of my hotel.

ETHELINE
(*pause*)

You're a bastard.

Royal nods. Etheline stares at him angrily, with tears in her eyes.

ETHELINE

Goodbye, Royal.

Royal turns and walks down the stairs.

INT. STAIRWELL. DAY

Chas stands at the bottom of the stairs and watches Royal come down with his suitcases. Royal stops in front of him.

ROYAL

Take it easy on those boys, Chassie. I don't want this to happen to you.

Chas hesitates. Royal walks past him and goes out the front door.

EXT. STREET. DAY

Richie and Royal stand on the sidewalk. Royal's suitcases are beside him. Margot and Henry stand at the top of the steps, in the front doorway.

ROYAL

You know, Richie, this illness, this closeness to death. It's been very profound for me. I feel like a different person. I really do.

RICHIE

Dad. You were never dying.

ROYAL
(*smiles*)

But I'm going to live.

Richie shakes his head. He turns away and goes up the steps, past Margot and Henry, into the house. Royal and Margot look at each other. Royal points to Henry.

ROYAL

He's not your father.

MARGOT
(*pause*)
Neither are you.

Margot closes the door. Royal puts his hands in his pockets. He stares into space. He begins to cry. A gypsy cab pulls over to the curb. Royal waves to the driver.

The front door of the house opens. Pagoda comes down the steps with two suitcases. He looks furious.

ROYAL
How you doing, pal?

Pagoda drops his suitcases on the ground.

PAGODA
You son of a bitch.

Pagoda's teeth flash as he goes over to Royal and stabs him with a penknife. Royal screams. He clutches his side. He falls on the ground. The gypsy cab driver watches blankly.

ROYAL
Goddammit! That's the last time I get knifed by you! You hear me?

Pagoda helps Royal to his feet. He collects his suitcases. Royal leans on Pagoda as they get into the gypsy cab. Royal says to the driver:

ROYAL
The 375th Street Y, please.

INSERT:

Page 198 of The Royal Tenenbaums. *It says Chapter Seven.*

EXT. 375TH STREET Y. DAY

A huge building that looks like a castle. A sign next to the door says 375th Street Y.

INT. 375TH STREET Y. DAY

An extremely small room with a low ceiling and a single bed. Royal stands in front of a mirror while Pagoda stitches up the knife-wound in his side. He holds a bottle of iodine in one hand and a box of bandages in the other.

> ROYAL

Everyone's against me.

> PAGODA

You can't blame them, man.

> ROYAL

I know. But, dammit, I want to be loved by this family.

Pagoda pours some iodine on a cotton ball and applies it to Royal's knife-wound. Royal grimaces.

> ROYAL

How much money you got?

> PAGODA

I don't have.

> ROYAL
> (*frowns*)

What do you mean? You're broke?

Pagoda nods. Royal looks furious.

> ROYAL

You got to be kidding me. How're we supposed to pay for the damn room?

Pagoda looks up at Royal coldly. Silence.

> ROYAL

All right. We'll figure something out.

INT. HENRY'S APARTMENT. NIGHT

Henry's bedroom is filled with paintings and sculptures from the fifties and sixties. He puts on a slow jazz record and sits down across from Etheline at a small table with a vase of roses, two bottles of wine, and three candles on it.

Henry has on pale-blue silk pyjamas. Etheline wears a cream silk nightgown. The doors to the balcony are open, and there is a gentle breeze. They look at each other fondly for a minute.

HENRY

Would you like another glass of wine?

ETHELINE

Yes, please.

Henry refills Etheline's glass. He clinks his glass against hers and takes a small sip. She drinks her whole glass all at once. Henry looks uneasy. Etheline says suddenly:

ETHELINE

Maybe we're rushing things, Henry.

HENRY
(*relieved*)

You're right. It's awkward sitting here in our pyjamas and everything. We don't have to do this right now. Let's just try to have a nice time.

ETHELINE

OK.

Henry gets up and changes the record to a more upbeat number.

HENRY

Yes, I think we're both a little uneasy, and there's no need for us to force anything. There's no hurry. Let's just –

ETHELINE

Actually, I should go.

Silence. Henry nods. He looks disappointed.

HENRY

Can I, at least, offer you some dessert?

Henry points to a dessert cart with a lemon meringue pie, two cheesecakes, a bowl of strawberries, a chocolate mousse, and a crêpe suzette on it. Etheline hesitates. Henry quickly strikes a match and sets the crêpe suzette on fire. His napkin catches on fire, and he dips it in his water glass. He looks to Etheline.

ETHELINE

No, I think you're right. I should go.

Etheline picks up her overnight bag off a chair and goes into the bathroom. Henry sits alone. He gets up and turns off the record player.

EXT. BRIDGE. DAY

A footbridge over the river. Margot waits in the middle of the bridge. Eli walks towards her from the opposite bank. His face is smeared with dirt and traces of paint. His clothes look severely dishevelled. He stops a few feet away from Margot.

> ELI
> I'm not in love with you any more.

> MARGOT
> I didn't know you ever were.

> ELI
> Let's not make this any more difficult than it already is.

> MARGOT
> (*pause*)

OK.

> ELI

OK, what?

> MARGOT
> OK, I'm not in love with you, either.

> ELI
> I know. You're in love with Richie. Which is sick and gross.

Silence. Margot nods.

> MARGOT
> Do you send my mother your clippings?

Eli hesitates.

> MARGOT
> And your grades in –

> ELI
> Please, stop ridiculing me.

Eli turns away and looks sadly out at the river. Margot goes over and stands beside him.

ELI

You never gave me the time of day until I started getting good reviews.

MARGOT

Your reviews aren't that good.

ELI

But the sales are.

CUT TO:

A second bridge, two hundred yards away. A large man in a coat and tie takes photographs of Margot and Eli with a telephoto lens.

INT. PRIVATE DETECTIVE'S OFFICE. DAY

A small room on the thirtieth floor of an office building. Raleigh, Richie and Dudley sit across a desk from the large man in the coat and tie. He is a detective.

DETECTIVE

How much do you already know, gentlemen?

RALEIGH

Very little, I assure you.

DETECTIVE

Would you like to examine the report?

RALEIGH

We would, rather. Yes.

The detective hands Raleigh a manilla folder. He opens it and begins to read. Richie looks over his shoulder.

MONTAGE:

Margot at age twelve buys a pack of cigarettes in a bodega.

She smokes one on the roof of the house, leaning against the chimney, next to the falcon's coop.

In each of the following images Margot smokes a cigarette.

AGE 21
RIVE GAUCHE

Margot climbs out the window of a girls' dormitory. She carries a small suitcase. She shimmies down the gutter and runs across the lawn.

Margot stands inside a torch-lit shack among a group of dancing Rastafarians in Jamaica. She holds hands with one of them while he lights a large, brown-paper-wrapped marijuana cigarette. A man dressed in a black shirt with a priest's collar places a string of shells around Margot's neck. Another man has a small machine gun. There is a goat in the doorway, and the ocean glimmers outside.

Margot opens a window and looks out at the Eiffel Tower. She wears a bra and a slip. A topless girl appears next to her, eating a croissant. The girl puts her arms around Margot's waist, and Margot runs her hands through the girl's hair.

CROSSTOWN LOCAL
AGE 27

Margot stands in a pool of water facing a young tribesman in New Guinea. He has on warpaint and wears a large tusk in his nose. Margot kisses him on the mouth.

Margot sits in a make-up chair at a television studio. Peter Bradley comes up behind her and puts his hands down her shirt. Margot smiles at him mischievously.

Margot makes out with
– a Puerto Rican teenager in the back seat of a taxi;
– a skinny guy with a mohawk on a city bus;
– a tough-looking Irishman on the deck of a ferry;
– Eli in a deserted subway train going full speed at night.

CUT TO:

Raleigh turning to the last page of the report. He closes the folder and looks to Richie. Richie looks stunned. Silence.

> RALEIGH

She smokes.

> DETECTIVE

Yes.

INT. BASEMENT. DAY

Royal, Pagoda, Dusty and the manager of the hotel sit at a table in the laundry room of the Lindbergh Palace. The manager is reviewing a typewritten document.

> MANAGER

All right. Everything seems to be in order. I'll contact you in the next twenty-four hours.

> ROYAL

I appreciate that. Which way are you leaning, by the way?

> MANAGER

I'll inform you of my decision at the appropriate time.

> ROYAL

I get it. Put in a good word for us, Dusty.

DUSTY
I already did.

INT. RALEIGH'S LABORATORY. DAY

Raleigh lies face down on the couch with his head buried in the cushions. Dudley walks over to him with a box of building blocks. He says quietly:

DUDLEY
You want to play some word games or do some experiments on me or anything?

Raleigh answers without moving. His voice is muffled.

RALEIGH
No.

Richie walks by in a bathrobe. He carries a pair of scissors. He goes into the bathroom, closes the door, and locks it.

INT. BATHROOM. DAY

Hot water runs full blast in the shower and the sink. Richie stands in the mirror. He holds a pair of scissors in his hand. He has clipped off his beard.

He opens the medicine cabinet and takes out a can of shaving cream and a straight razor. He covers his face with shaving cream. He picks up the razor. He looks back in the mirror. He pushes his hand back through his hair, takes a deep breath, and says quietly:

RICHIE
I'm going to kill myself tomorrow.

Silence. Richie slices the razor deeply, four times, along his left forearm. Blood runs into the sink. He switches hands with the razor and slashes his other wrist. He sits down on the floor.

CUT TO:

The bathroom door slamming open. Dudley bursts into the room. He looks horrified. The floor is flooded with water and blood. Richie is slumped in the corner with shaving cream all over his face.

Dudley screams hysterically.

MONTAGE:

Three paramedics race down a corridor pushing Richie on a gurney. Raleigh and Dudley run beside them. They are covered with blood.

Etheline hangs up the telephone and runs into the hallway. She throws open the closet door and grabs her coat.

Chas, Ari and Uzi hold on as Anwar weaves the B.M.W. in and out of traffic. Buckley has his head out the window.

Margot bursts through the doors of the emergency room. She looks around frantically. She sees Dudley. She sees the blood on him. She rushes over and grabs his arms.

> MARGOT
> Where is he, Dudley?

> DUDLEY
> (*pause*)
> Who?

INT. HOSPITAL ROOM. DAY

Everyone is gathered around Richie in his hospital bed. His arms are covered with bandages. A doctor gives him an injection and says to Etheline:

> DOCTOR
> He'll probably sleep for several hours, and then I'll come back to check on him.

Etheline nods. She has tears all over her face. The doctor leaves the room. Margot holds Richie's hand.

> MARGOT
> How do you feel?

> RICHIE
> Fine, thanks.

> ETHELINE
> Are you in any pain?

                    RICHIE
Not really.

                    CHAS
Why'd you try to kill yourself?

                    ETHELINE
Don't press him right now.

                    RICHIE
I wrote a suicide note.

                    MARGOT
You did?

                    RICHIE
Yeah. Right after I regained consciousness.

Everyone looks slightly confused.

                    CHAS
Can we read it?

                    RICHIE
No.

                    CHAS
Could you paraphrase it for us?

                    RICHIE
I don't think so.

                    CHAS
Is it dark?

                    RICHIE
Of course it's dark. It's a suicide note.

                    ETHELINE
All right. That's enough. The doctor said to let him sleep.

INT. WAITING AREA. DAY

The corridor outside Richie's room. Etheline fills out some insurance forms. Ari and Uzi sit on Chas' lap. Margot sits next to Raleigh. Raleigh stares into space.

RALEIGH

You've made a cuckold of me.

Everyone looks to Raleigh and Margot. Silence.

MARGOT

I know.

RALEIGH

Many times over.

MARGOT

I'm sorry.

RALEIGH

And you've nearly killed your poor brother.

ETHELINE

What's he talking about?

MARGOT

It doesn't matter.

RALEIGH

She's balling Eli Cash.

Everyone looks surprised and extremely uncomfortable.

ETHELINE

Oh, my goodness.

RALEIGH

May I have a cigarette?

MARGOT

What?

RALEIGH

Shall I repeat the question?

MARGOT

You don't smoke.

RALEIGH
(*bitterly*)

I bloody well know that.

Raleigh stares at Margot in silence. Margot sighs. She reaches into her pocket and takes out a pack of cigarettes. She gives one to Raleigh. He puts it in his mouth.

RALEIGH

And a light, please?

Margot takes out some matches and lights Raleigh's cigarette.

RALEIGH

Thank you.

Raleigh stands up and walks away, down the hall, out the door. Silence. Margot lights a cigarette for herself. Etheline looks disturbed.

ETHELINE

How long have you been a smoker?

MARGOT
(*pause*)

Twenty-two years.

ETHELINE

Well, I think you should quit.

Margot nods.

The door opens at the end of the hall. Henry Sherman comes in. Etheline sees him and stands up. He goes over to her. He starts to put on his glasses. As he unfolds them, he unintentionally clamps them on to his necktie and pulls his necktie up to his temple. He says earnestly:

HENRY

How can I help?

Etheline begins to point to Henry's necktie suspended near his ear, but she hesitates. Henry senses something wrong in his peripheral vision and looks confused. He swats at the necktie, hurling his glasses off his face and on to the floor.

Henry picks up his glasses and puts them back on. He looks to Etheline with an embarrassed expression. Etheline puts her arms around him. She hugs him tightly and starts to cry.

EXT. STREET. NIGHT

Three hours later. A gypsy cab stops in front of the hospital. Royal and Pagoda get out and walk quickly into the building. They are both dressed in hotel elevator-operator uniforms.

INT. HOSPITAL. NIGHT

Royal speaks anxiously to a nurse at the registration desk. Pagoda stands behind him.

                    ROYAL

Richie Tenenbaum, please.

                    NURSE

Your name?

                    ROYAL

Royal Tenenbaum.

The nurse looks down at her registration book. She frowns. She looks back to Royal.

                    NURSE

I'm afraid visiting hours are over, sir.

                    ROYAL
                 (*hesitates*)

Why? What does it say there? They don't want me?

                    NURSE

I'm sorry. I have to refer you to Dr Burroughs. He'll be in tomorrow afternoon.

Silence.

EXT. SIDEWALK. NIGHT

Royal and Pagoda stand in front of the hospital. Royal points to the edge of the roof. He sounds desperate.

                    ROYAL

I think if we shimmy up that gutter and jump across the window ledge we can pry open the ventilation shaft and –

                    PAGODA

There he is, man.

Pagoda points to Richie waiting at the bus stop on the corner. He is dressed in surgical scrubs and bedroom slippers. His arms are covered with bandages. Royal looks puzzled. A bus pulls over in front of Richie. The doors open. Royal calls out:

                    ROYAL

Richie?

Richie looks to Royal and Pagoda. He sees their uniforms. He hesitates.

ROYAL

Where're you going?

Silence. Richie gets on the bus. Royal and Pagoda watch it drive away. Royal looks very upset.

ROYAL

I have to say, he didn't look half bad for a suicide. Attempted suicide, anyway.

Pagoda nods. He puts his arm around Royal's shoulder.

INT. BUS. NIGHT

An old city bus with trash on the floor and graffiti spray-painted on the walls. Richie sits in the back row and rides downtown.

INT. BALLROOM. NIGHT

The ballroom on the top floor of the Tenenbaum house. Richie walks in and sees the lamp glowing inside his tent. Margot calls out from inside:

MARGOT

Who's there?

Richie does not respond.

MARGOT

Hello?

Richie looks at the seventeen paintings of Margot hanging in the corner. An unfinished eighteenth, with Margot slightly older, leans against the wall. Richie goes to the tent at the centre of the room.

INT. TENT. NIGHT

Richie looks into the tent. Margot is sitting on the floor next to a record player smoking a cigarette. She has a Rolling Stones record in her hand. She looks startled.

RICHIE

What are you doing in my tent?

MARGOT
(*hesitates*)

Just listening to some records.

Margot puts out her cigarette. She seems worried.

> MARGOT
> I thought you were supposed to be in the hospital.

> RICHIE
> I checked myself out.

> MARGOT
> Well, shouldn't you be on some kind of suicide watch or something?

> RICHIE
> (*pause*)

Probably.

Richie goes into the tent and sits down Indian-style in front of Margot. Margot sighs. She puts on the Rolling Stones record. It plays quietly.

> MARGOT
> How many stitches did you get?

> RICHIE
> I don't know. You want to see?

Margot nods. Richie unwraps one of the bandages. His arm is covered with jagged, criss-crossing stitches and dried blood. Margot looks stricken.

> MARGOT
> Jesus, Richie. That looks horrible.

Richie nods. He wraps the bandage back around his arm.

> RICHIE
>
> I heard about your ex-husband.

> MARGOT
> (*pause*)

Desmond?

> RICHIE
> (*hesitates*)
> I guess so. I didn't get his name.

> MARGOT
>
> Yeah. I met him in the ocean. I was swimming, and he came out to me in a canoe. We were only married for nine days.

> RICHIE
> (*nods*)

And I heard about Eli.

> MARGOT
> (*sighs*)
> I know. Poor Eli. Anyway, we mostly just talked about you.

> RICHIE
> (*surprised*)

You did?

> MARGOT
>
> Yeah. I guess that was the attraction, if you know what I mean.

Silence. Richie says quietly:

> RICHIE
>
> I have to tell you something.

> MARGOT

What's that?

> RICHIE

I love you.

MARGOT
(*sadly*)

I love you, too.

Richie kisses Margot on the mouth, and she kisses him back. She puts her hands on the back of his head. Richie pulls away from her and looks into her eyes.

RICHIE

I can't stop thinking about you. I went away for a year, and it only got worse. I don't know what to do.

MARGOT

Let's lie down for a minute.

Richie lies down on the cot. Margot looks at his Boy Scout sleeping bag.

MARGOT

This is the one we took to the museum, isn't it?

Richie nods. Margot sighs. She lies down next to Richie and puts her arm around his shoulder. She smoothes back his hair. They listen to the music for a minute.

MARGOT

Why'd you do it? Because of me?

RICHIE

Yeah, but it's not your fault.

MARGOT

You're not going to do it again, are you?

RICHIE
(*pause*)

I doubt it.

Margot nods. She starts crying. She kisses Richie's hand. Richie looks worried. Margot gets up and goes out the tent. Richie sits alone for a minute. Margot looks back into the tent.

MARGOT

I think we're just going to have to be secretly in love with each other and leave it at that, Richie.

They look at each other for a long minute. Richie nods. Margot turns away and goes out the tent.

Richie picks up the stack of books off the table next to his cot. The book on top is Family of Geniuses. *Then there are Margot's book, Raleigh's book, Henry's book and Eli's book. He spreads them out on the floor among his Matchbox cars and tennis trophies. A dalmatian mouse appears and crawls among them. The record ends.*

INSERT:

Page 230 of The Royal Tenenbaums. *It says Chapter Eight.*

INT. HALLWAY. DAY

The next morning. Richie comes downstairs in his pyjamas. He carries the stuffed boar's head. He hangs it on the wall in its place.

INT. ELEVATOR. DAY

The elevator at the Lindbergh Palace. Royal is dressed in his elevator-operator uniform. He takes three well-dressed businessmen down to the lobby. He looks exhausted and depressed. The doors open. One of the businessmen hands Royal a dollar as they walk out into the lobby.

> ROYAL
> Thank you, sir.

Royal sees Richie standing in front of the elevator. Royal looks surprised. The doors of another elevator open. Pagoda is the operator. Richie looks at him. Pagoda hesitates. He waves to Richie. Richie waves back.

> ROYAL
> Going up?

Richie looks back to Royal. He nods. He steps into Royal's elevator.

> ROYAL
> What floor?

> RICHIE
> It doesn't matter.

Royal closes the doors and pulls a lever. The elevator goes up. Royal stands with his back to Richie.

>   RICHIE
> So you're elevator operators now.

>   ROYAL
> Yeah. We just started, but we'll get a bump when we join the union.

>   RICHIE
> What made you decide to do that?

>   ROYAL
> Well, we're broke. But, in answer to your question, I guess I'm trying to prove I can pay my dues and what-not. I just hope somebody notices.

Richie nods. Silence.

>   RICHIE
> You asked me why I choked out there that day.

Royal turns around quickly and looks to Richie. He nods.

>   RICHIE
> Well, I think I know the answer, and I wanted your advice.

Royal looks surprised and moved. He says quietly:

>   ROYAL
> Sure.

EXT. ROOF. DAY

Royal and Richie stand at the edge of the roof, looking out at the city. Silence.

> ROYAL

Margot Tenenbaum?

> RICHIE

Yeah.

> ROYAL

Since when?

> RICHIE

Since always.

> ROYAL

Does she know?

> RICHIE

Uh-huh.

> ROYAL

And what's her feeling about it?

> RICHIE

I think she feels confused.

> ROYAL

I can understand that. It's probably illegal.

> RICHIE

I don't think so. We're not related by blood.

> ROYAL
> (*pause*)

That's true.

Silence. Royal nods.

> ROYAL

It's still frowned upon, but then what isn't these days, right?

Richie nods. Royal shrugs.

ROYAL

I don't know. Maybe it works. Why not? Hell, you love each
other, and nobody knows what's going to happen, so –

Royal stops short. His expression changes.

ROYAL

You know what? Don't listen to me. I never understood
her, myself. I never understood any of us. I wish I knew
what to tell you, but I just don't.

RICHIE
(*pause*)

That's OK.

ROYAL

No, it's not.

*Royal looks very sad. He stares down at the ground. He takes a deep
breath. He says quietly:*

ROYAL

Do you still consider me your father?

RICHIE

Sure, I do.

ROYAL

I wish I had a little more to offer in that department.

RICHIE

I know you do, Pop.

Royal nods. He keeps looking down at the ground.

ROYAL

I don't blame you, by the way.

Richie looks off into the distance. He frowns.

ROYAL

She's a great-looking girl, and she's smart as whip, and –

RICHIE

Mordecai?

Royal looks up. A falcon flies in a low circle around the building. Royal and Richie watch as it lands on the railing in front of them. Silence.

ROYAL

Holy shit.

Richie slowly reaches out to the falcon. He smoothes out the feathers on its neck and says softly:

RICHIE

You came back.

Royal looks up at the sky. He seems frightened.

ROYAL
Jiminy Cricket. He must have a goddamn radar in his brain.

Richie frowns. He hesitates.

RICHIE
I'm not so sure this is Mordecai.

ROYAL
What do you mean? He flew right in here.

RICHIE
Yeah, but now he has white feathers on his neck.

Royal and Richie study the falcon. Richie seems uncertain.

ROYAL
Well, the son of a bitch must be moulting.

INT. ELEVATOR. DAY

Richie and Royal ride down in the elevator. The falcon is perched on Richie's arm.

RICHIE
I need your help with something else.

ROYAL
(*excitedly*)
You got it. What's the situation?

RICHIE

Well, I think –

ROYAL

Hang on.

Royal throws the lever on the elevator to full speed. It accelerates and starts shaking violently. He yells into a walkie-talkie:

ROYAL

Pagoda! Let's hit it!

RICHIE
(*hesitates*)
I didn't mean right this second.

INT. ELI'S STUDY. DAY

Eli sits on the couch in his study working on a jigsaw puzzle of the Beatles crossing Abbey Road. Three Egyptian men are chopping up yellow powder on the table. Electronic music blasts from the stereo.

There is a knock on the door. Everyone looks up. Silence.

ELI

Yes?

The door opens and Richie looks inside. Eli and the Egyptian men stare at Richie. Eli has yellow powder on his nose. He says awkwardly:

ELI

Hey, Richie.

Richie walks into the room. Royal and Pagoda follow him. They are dressed in their elevator-operator uniforms. Eli looks confused and uneasy.

RICHIE

We want to take you to get some help.

ELI
(*pause*)

Is it just you guys?

Richie looks slightly confused.

                              ELI
    I guess Margot and your mother couldn't make it.

Eli looks disappointed. He sees the bandages wrapped around Richie's
arms.

                              ELI
    What happened there?

                            RICHIE
                           (*hesitates*)
    Nothing.

Royal looks to the Egyptian men.

                             ROYAL
    Would you excuse us, please?

The Egyptian men hesitate. Pagoda points to the door. The Egyptian
men leave the room.

                            RICHIE
    Where's Sabrina?

                              ELI
                           (*pause*)
    They went back to England.

Richie nods. He sits down next to Eli. Royal and Pagoda sit across
from them.

                            RICHIE
    Are we still friends?

Eli seems embarrassed and hurt.

                              ELI
    What do you mean?

                            RICHIE
    Are we?

                              ELI
    Of course. I can't believe you would ask me that.

                            RICHIE
    It doesn't matter. I heard about you and Margot.

Silence. Eli gets up and goes over to the window. He looks out at the backyard. Richie goes over and stands next to him. Eli looks deeply depressed.

>   ELI
> I'm sorry. I don't know what to say.

>   RICHIE
> You don't have to say anything.

>   ELI
> I always wanted to be a Tenenbaum, you know?

Richie nods. Eli looks to Royal. Royal nods and says quietly:

>   ROYAL
> Me, too. Me, too.

>   ELI
> But it doesn't mean what it used to, does it?

Richie shakes his head. Eli opens the window, reaches out, and picks a dead leaf off the branch of a tree. He looks to Richie.

>   ELI
> I wish you'd've done this for me when I was a kid.

>   RICHIE
>   (*pause*)
> But you didn't have a drug problem then.

>   ELI
> Yeah, but it still would've meant a lot to me. Anyway, I really
> appreciate you coming over here now. I do recognize that
> I have a problem, and I want to get better. Let me just get
> my things.

Eli goes into the bathroom and locks the door. Pagoda goes over to the window and looks out.

He sees Eli running down the fire escape.

>   PAGODA
> There he goes.

Royal and Richie rush over to the window. They watch Eli drop to the ground, run into the street, and hail a taxi. He has on socks but no shoes.

INT. ICE-CREAM PARLOUR. DAY

A room decorated like a birthday cake. Every booth is filled with divorced fathers and their young daughters. Margot sits across from Royal. Royal is dressed in his elevator-operator uniform. A waiter stands next to them.

> ROYAL
>
> I want to order some ice cream for my daughter, please. What would you like, Margot?

> MARGOT
>
> I told you. Nothing. I only have five minutes.

Royal looks frustrated. Margot sighs.

> MARGOT
>
> I'll have a butterscotch sundae, I guess.

The waiter nods and walks away. Silence.

> ROYAL
>
> Your brother's all torn up inside.

> MARGOT
> *(hesitates)*
>
> Well, so am I, but I'm not going to discuss it with you.

Royal sighs. He leans across the table and says urgently:

> ROYAL
>
> Can't somebody be a shit their whole life and want to repair the damage? I mean, I think people want to hear that.

> MARGOT
>
> Do they?

Royal nods. Silence.

> MARGOT
>
> You probably don't even know my middle name.

> ROYAL
> *(pause)*
>
> It's a trick question. You don't have one.

MARGOT

Helen.

ROYAL
(*surprised*)
That was my mother's name.

MARGOT
(*sadly*)
I know it was.

EXT. SIDEWALK. DAY

Royal stands on the sidewalk in front of the Tenenbaum house. He has a bunch of white flowers in his hand. Anwar is asleep in the B.M.W. parked at the kerb. Royal throws a pebble at a window on the third floor.

Ari looks out the window. Royal smiles. Ari opens the window. Uzi appears beside him. Royal calls up to them:

ROYAL
Anybody feel like grabbing a couple of burgers and hitting the cemetery?

Chas appears between Ari and Uzi. He looks down at Royal. Royal looks nervous. Chas closes the window.

CUT TO:

Royal putting his bunch of flowers on Rachael's grave. He stands alone with his hands in his pockets. He walks away.

EXT. STREET. DAY

Etheline and Henry come down the front steps of Henry's building. They both look depressed. Royal is waiting at the bus stop on the corner, next to a small Mexican man in a windbreaker and a tie. Royal has a large envelope in his hands. Etheline and Henry see him. Royal goes over to them.

ROYAL
I got you something, Ethel. Actually, I made it.

Etheline and Henry look at Royal warily. Royal hands Etheline the envelope. She looks to Henry. Henry shrugs. She opens the envelope. It contains a sheaf of typewritten documents.

ETHELINE

What's this?

ROYAL

A divorce.

Etheline looks to Royal. She says quietly:

ETHELINE

From you?

ROYAL

Yes.

Royal looks to Henry. Henry does not know what to say. Royal motions to the Mexican man.

ROYAL

This is Sanchez. He's a notary public.

HENRY
(*hesitates*)

Hello.

SANCHEZ

Hello, sir.

ROYAL

If you'll just sign here, please, Ethel.

Royal hands Etheline a pen and points to a dotted line. Etheline signs.

ROYAL

And here.

Etheline signs.

ROYAL

And initial here.

Etheline signs. Royal hands the sheaf of documents to Sanchez. Sanchez puts several stamps and notations on it. Royal looks up at Henry's building.

ROYAL

You own this building, don't you, Henry? It's magnificent.
I used to be a home-owner myself, but my son expropriated
it from me.

Henry does not respond. A city bus approaches from the next block.

ROYAL

Here comes my bus. Thanks, Sanchez.

SANCHEZ

You're welcome.

ETHELINE

Are we divorced?

ROYAL

Almost. Sanchez just has to file the papers.

Royal signals to the bus driver.

ROYAL

I love you, Etheline. And congratulations, both of you.

Royal looks to Henry. He turns back to Etheline.

ROYAL

I didn't think so much of him at first, but now I get it. He's
everything I'm not.

*Royal smiles. He turns away suddenly, runs to the bus, and jumps
inside. He looks back to Etheline. He yells:*

ROYAL

Take back Pagoda, will you?

*Etheline hesitates. She nods. The door closes. Etheline and Henry stand
watching with Sanchez.*

INT. ELI'S CAR. NIGHT

*Eli drives through a tunnel at top speed in the middle of the night.
He has on sunglasses, and he is covered with grass and dirt. Electronic
music blasts from the stereo. He looks lost and sad.*

CUT TO:

Page 258. It says Chapter Nine.

INSERT:

An invitation to Etheline and Henry's wedding at the house on Archer Avenue. It is nearly identical to the invitation on the cover of the first edition of The Royal Tenenbaums.

EXT. STREET. DAY

Ari, Uzi and Pagoda stand in front of the house with Buckley, receiving the wedding guests. They help people out of their cars, give them programmes for the ceremony, and direct them to the front door.

There are about fifty guests. Half of them are black and half are white. The members of the wedding party are dressed in morning suits.

Royal and Dusty get out of a gypsy cab. Royal smiles at Ari and Uzi. He hugs Pagoda and kisses Ari and Uzi on the tops of their heads. He looks around. He whispers:

> ROYAL
>
> I got you some jawbreakers.

Royal slips Ari and Uzi each a large purple-and-green-striped jawbreaker. They hide them in their jackets.

INT. CHAS' BEDROOM. DAY

A twenty-one-year-old black Navy midshipman helps Henry finish tying his bow tie. The midshipman is Walter. Henry studies his tie in the mirror.

> HENRY
>
> It's slightly uneven.

Henry unties his knot and starts from scratch. Richie cracks open the door and looks into the room.

> RICHIE
>
> Henry?

Henry looks to the door.

HENRY

Hello, Richie. This is my son, Walter Sherman.

Richie comes into the room. He and Walter shake hands.

RICHIE

Nice to meet you, Walter.

WALTER

Nice to meet you.

CHAS

Henry's your dad?

Chas is standing in the doorway. Walter hesitates. He nods. Chas looks to Henry.

CHAS

So you've been married before?

HENRY

Yes. I'm a widower.

CHAS

Oh, yeah. I forgot.

Pause.

You know, I'm a widower myself.

HENRY

I know you are, Chas.

INT. MARGOT'S BEDROOM. DAY

Margot looks out the window at the guests arriving on the street while Etheline finishes her make-up. Margot has a white plastic inhaler in her mouth.

ETHELINE

What are you chewing on?

MARGOT

My nicotine inhaler. It's supposed to help me quit.

ETHELINE

Is it working?

134

MARGOT

Not really.

EXT. STREET. DAY

Ari and Uzi tie Buckley's leash around a pole in front of the house. Royal and a very small Irish priest stand together at the top of the steps.

ROYAL

Well, of course, I'm half Hebrew, but the children are three-quarters Mick-Catholic.

PRIEST
(*nods*)
So they were raised in the Church.

ROYAL
(*pause*)
I believe so. I really don't know.

A car's tyres squeal around the corner. Royal and the priest look down the block. Eli's convertible skids through the turn on to Archer Avenue. Royal and the priest frown.

INT. ELI'S CAR. DAY

Eli's face is covered with Apache warpaint. He is dressed in a morning suit. He wears a distracted smile. He downshifts, accelerates, and steers toward the Tenenbaum house. He whispers:

ELI

Here I come.

CUT TO:

Ari, Uzi and Buckley watching frozen as Eli's car races towards them. Royal looks panicked. He looks to Ari and Uzi and hollers:

ROYAL

Boys!

Royal jumps down the stairs.

INT. MARGOT'S BEDROOM. DAY

There is a tremendous crashing boom and the sound of shattering glass. Etheline rushes over next to Margot at the window.

ETHELINE

What was that?

MARGOT

Eli just crashed his car into the front of the house.

ETHELINE

Oh, my God.

INT. STAIRWELL. DAY

Chas sprints down the stairs three at a time. He falls and bangs against the wall. He gets back up and keeps running.

INT. LIVING ROOM. DAY

Eli sits on the floor, barefoot, covered in glass and debris. He is bleeding from a head wound. Three dalmatian mice dart around the room in confusion. Several guests help Eli stagger to his feet. They look alarmed at his appearance, particularly the warpaint.

ELI

Where are my shoes?

Dudley finds one of Eli's shoes in the fireplace. He hands it to Eli. Eli puts it on.

EXT. SIDEWALK. DAY

The wedding guests quickly begin to come out the front door and gather around the smashed car. There is also a crushed mailbox, and mail is scattered all over the sidewalk. The lighter airmail envelopes drift about in the wind. Chas runs down the steps. He yells:

CHAS

Where are you?

Royal and Richie stand up among the rubble. Royal holds Ari under one arm and Uzi under the other. He sets them down. Chas runs over to them.

ROYAL

They're OK, Chas.

Chas grabs Ari and Uzi. He examines them.

ROYAL

It's OK. They're safe.

ARI

Dad, they ran over Buckley.

CHAS

What?

Chas looks to Royal. Royal nods. He turns to the wreckage. Buckley's leash remains tied to the railing and extends taut beneath the wheels of Eli's car.

ROYAL

I think we lost Buckley.

Ari and Uzi start to cry. Richie brushes some debris off Uzi's hair. He looks to Chas and points to Royal.

RICHIE

He saved them. Kind of.

Chas looks to Richie. He says blankly:

CHAS

He did?

Richie nods. Chas looks to Royal. Royal shrugs. Eli appears in the broken front window of the house.

ELI

Did I hit anybody?

Everyone looks to Eli.

ELI

Is everybody OK?

Eli sees Chas staring at him. Eli hesitates. He darts away from the window. Chas bolts up the steps, banging his way through the crowd.

ROYAL

Chas! Wait!

INT. HALLWAY. DAY

Chas bursts into the house. He screams:

                              CHAS
    Eli!

The guests panic as Eli jumps over a couch, knocks over a chair, and ducks into the kitchen.

INT. KITCHEN. DAY

Pagoda looks up from a tray of canapés he is preparing. He does not appear to notice Eli's strange appearance and injuries. He holds out one of the canapés to him.

                              PAGODA
    This is the quail's egg.

Eli takes it quickly. Chas smashes open the door. Eli body-checks him and breaks out of the room. They slam past the priest and knock him down the basement stairs. The wedding guests scream and yell and try to break it up or get away.

Eli slips out the back door and sprints into the garden.

EXT. BACKYARD. DAY

Eli runs to the back wall and tries the gate. It is locked. Chas tackles him hard. Chas grabs him by the arm, swings him around, and slams him against the wall. Eli yells. People rush into the backyard. Richie runs outside.

                              RICHIE
    Chas! Don't!

Richie tries to pull Chas off Eli. Chas elbows Richie in the face. Richie falls backwards into the bushes. Chas picks up Eli and tries to throw him over the wall. Eli scratches and clutches.

                              ELI
    Help! Please!

Chas yells insanely. He throws Eli over the wall. He turns to everyone watching him. They look stunned. Chas breathes heavily. Richie sits up in the bushes. He has his hand over his eye.

Chas?

Chas hesitates. He climbs over the wall.

EXT. NEIGHBOUR'S YARD. DAY

Chas lands in a Zen garden, next to Eli. Eli is stretched out on his back. He and Chas look at each other. Chas lies down on the ground. He seems drained. It is very quiet. They both stare up at the sky. There are bonsai trees all around them.

ELI
Did I hit the dog?

CHAS
Yeah.

ELI
(pause)
Is he dead?

CHAS
Yeah.

ELI
(pause)
I need help.

CHAS
So do I.

Walter looks over the top of the wall, down at Chas and Eli. He looks back behind him and yells to someone:

WALTER
Go around to the other side!

EXT. EMBASSY. DAY

Henry and Royal run around the corner and up the steps of a neighbour's house. A plaque next to the front door says Residence of the Japanese Ambassador. Royal knocks. They wait. Royal looks to Henry. He says suddenly:

Can I say something to you, Henry?

Henry looks to Royal.

ROYAL

I've been considered an asshole for about as long as I can remember. That's just my style. But I'd feel pretty blue if I didn't think you were going to forgive me.

Henry nods. He says gently:

HENRY

I don't think you're an asshole, Royal. You're just a kind of a son of a bitch.

Royal seems genuinely moved by this remark.

ROYAL

Well, I appreciate that.

The door opens. A small Asian woman in a kimono looks out at them.

ROYAL

Can we get into your backyard, ma'am? We got a couple of boys out there.

EXT. SIDEWALK. DAY

There are two police cars, an ambulance, a tow-truck and a fire-engine in front of the house. Raleigh and two paramedics roll the priest on a gurney. Raleigh holds the priest's hand.

PARAMEDIC

I think he may've broken his ankle.

RALEIGH

That's not terribly serious, is it? (*to the priest*) Do you have an alternative?

The priest shakes his head.

Eli is being questioned by a police officer. His warpaint is smeared, and there are several bandages on his head and arms. He looks very upset.

ELI

At which point I apparently lost control of the vehicle, smashed it into the house, and killed that poor dog.

The police officer studies Eli's driver's licence.

POLICE OFFICER

You're Eli Cash.

ELI
(pause)

I am, indeed.

POLICE OFFICER

I love your work.

ELI
(touched)

How sweet of you to say so.

Royal stands among a group of firemen with a dalmatian.

ROYAL

I think he's part mutt. What kind of papers you got for him?

One of the firemen shrugs. Royal points at the dalmatian.

ROYAL

Sparkplug. Sit.

The dalmatian sits. Royal looks impressed.

Dusty stands with Richie on the sidewalk and examines his eye. It is scratched badly and looks terrible.

DUSTY

Can you see out of it?

Richie covers his good eye to test his bad eye.

RICHIE

Not really.

DUSTY

Uh-huh. Minor corneal damage. Page me if it spreads to the other eye.

Raleigh and Dudley stand next to each other wearing firemen's helmets. Dudley laughs crazily.

                    RALEIGH
What's so funny, Dudley?

                    DUDLEY
You look great!

Henry and Walter survey the scene from the smashed-out living-room window. Walter points to the rubble.

                    WALTER
But these aren't structure-bearing elements, Dad.

                    HENRY
It doesn't matter. It's still best to file it under force majeure and recoup the deductible.

Ari and Uzi try to look at Buckley under Eli's car as several firemen and tow-truck drivers attach straps and chains to the wheels and axle. Etheline goes over to them.

                    ETHELINE
You boys come over here with me.

                    ARI
But Buckley's still under there.

                    ETHELINE
I know, but there's nothing we can do for him, at the moment.

Royal takes the dalmatian over to Chas.

                    ROYAL
I got you a new dog for the boys.

Chas looks at the dalmatian. He looks back to Royal.

                    CHAS
What's this?

                    ROYAL
I just bought him.

                              CHAS
     You did?

Royal nods. Silence.

                              ROYAL
     I'm sorry I let you down, Chas. All of you. I've been trying
     to make it up to you.

Royal holds out the leash. Chas hesitates. He takes it.

                              CHAS
     What's his name?

                              ROYAL
                            (*quietly*)
     Sparkplug.

                              CHAS
     Thank you.

                              ROYAL
     You're welcome.

Chas suddenly starts crying. He stares at the ground.

                              CHAS
     We've had a rough year, Dad.

                              ROYAL
     I know you have, Chassie.

*Royal puts his hand on Chas' head. Chas looks to Royal and takes a
deep breath. He nods. Royal watches as Chas takes the dalmatian over
to Ari and Uzi and talks to them quietly for a minute.*

*Uzi pets the dalmatian. Ari takes the leash. Etheline looks to Royal.
Royal looks back at her. Etheline smiles sadly.*

EXT. ROOF. DAY

*Richie and Margot sit near the edge of the roof, next to the falcon in
its coop. Richie has an ice pack over his eye. He brushes his hand
against the white feathers on the falcon's neck.*

MARGOT
I wonder what happened to him.

RICHIE
I don't know. (*Pause.*) Sometimes when people have a
traumatic experience, their hair turns white.

Silence. Margot says quietly:

MARGOT
Well, I'm sure he'll get over it.

*Richie nods. Margot looks at him for a minute. She takes her inhaler
out of her mouth and puts it in her pocket. She turns and looks at the
top of the chimney. She pulls out a loose brick. She reaches behind it
and takes out a pack of cigarettes and a matchbook. She looks to
Richie. She points at the chimney.*

MARGOT
This was one of my first hiding places.

*Richie studies the pack of cigarettes. It is still sealed, but the wrapper
looks faded.*

RICHIE
How old you think those are?

*Margot opens the pack, takes out a cigarette, puts it in her mouth, and
lights it. She takes a puff.*

MARGOT
I'd say about ten years.

Richie nods. Margot offers him a cigarette. He takes it, and she lights it. Margot puts her arm around Richie's shoulder, and they smoke their stale cigarettes together.

EXT. GARDEN. DAY

Ari, Uzi and Chas watch Royal throw dirt on to a grave in the backyard. They have tears in their eyes. The dalmatian sits on the ground next to them.

NARRATOR
Royal dug a hole for Buckley behind the garden shed, and buried him in a canvas duffel bag.

Chas hands Royal a bottle of scotch, and Royal takes a drink.

ROYAL
All right, boys. Say a prayer.

Ari begins, with a jawbreaker in his mouth:

ARI
Dear Heavenly Father –

INT. OFFICE. DAY

Henry and Etheline stand side by side in front of a judge in a small office with green carpet and an exercise bicycle. Henry has his left hand raised and his right hand on a Bible.

145

HENRY

So help me God.

The judge extends the Bible to Etheline. She puts her hand on it.

NARRATOR

Etheline and Henry were married forty-eight hours later, in judge's chambers.

INT. THEATRE. NIGHT

A stage-set for a play that appears to take place in a network of tree houses on a tropical island. A father introduces his daughter to a group of native tribesmen.

FATHER

This is my adopted daughter, Elaine Levinson.

The house is sold out. Royal sits in the front row with the other Tenenbaums. He laughs quietly and shakes his head. The rest of the audience is silent.

NARRATOR

Margot's new play, *The Levinsons in the Trees*, was produced at the Cavendish Theatre.

CUT TO

Margot standing alone outside the theatre, under the marquee, smoking a cigarette.

NARRATOR

It ran for just under two weeks and received mixed reviews.

INT. AUDITORIUM. DAY

Brooks College. Raleigh and Dudley sit onstage at a table in front of an audience of doctors and medical students. Raleigh takes a question.

MEDICAL STUDENT

Can he tell time?

RALEIGH

Oh, my Lord, no.

Dudley shakes his head emphatically.

NARRATOR

Raleigh and Dudley went on a lecture tour to eleven universities in the promotion of their new book.

INSERT:

A copy of Raleigh's new book, Dudley's World. *On the dust jacket there is a yearbook photograph of Dudley with his Henry Aaron-style glasses flipped up. His expression is almost impossibly blank.*

EXT. HOSPITAL. DAY

A resort compound on the high plains. Eli practises with a lasso in front of several young addicts. He has stitches on his forehead.

NARRATOR
Eli checked himself into a rehabilitation hospital in North Dakota.

A tall, skinny, Native American man in his late forties walks over to Eli. He and Eli are dressed in matching deerskin jackets. Eli points to him.

ELI
This is my sponsor, Runs with Two Horses.

INT. 375TH STREET Y ROOFTOP. DAY

A concrete tennis court with a chain-link net. Ari, Uzi and a group of children dressed in tennis clothes watch as Richie demonstrates the continental style of grip to them. Richie has a white gauze patch taped over his eye.

RICHIE
Rod Laver used it. You know who Laver is?

Uzi steps up to the service line. He bounces a ball and gets ready to serve.

NARRATOR
Richie started a programme teaching competitive tennis to eight- to twelve-year-olds at the 375th Street Y.

Uzi hits a fast serve to Richie's forehand. Richie fires his return full-speed straight down the line. Uzi watches it race past him.

EXT. STREET. DAY

Royal, Chas, Ari and Uzi ride on the back of a speeding garbage truck. They are all laughing.

NARRATOR
Royal had a heart attack at the age of sixty-eight.

INT. AMBULANCE. DAY

Royal is strapped on to a gurney with tubes sticking out of his arms and an oxygen mask on his face. Chas sits beside him, holding his hand. The ambulance races full-speed up the wrong side of the street.

NARRATOR

Chas rode with him in the ambulance, and was the only
witness to his father's death.

*Royal appears to be smiling underneath his oxygen mask. He looks up
at Chas. Chas puts his hand on Royal's cheek. Royal closes his eyes.*

NARRATOR

In his will, he stipulated that his funeral take place at dusk.

INSERT:

Page 275 of The Royal Tenenbaums. *It says Epilogue.*

EXT. CEMETERY. DAY

*Snow falls lightly, and the sky is getting dark. Everyone in the family
is gathered around as Chas, Richie, Henry, Raleigh, Eli, Dusty and
Pagoda lower the casket. They are all bundled up in coats and scarves.
They step away from the grave.*

*Henry stands next to Etheline. She takes his arm. Pagoda wears
Royal's sunglasses. Tears stream down his face. Dusty stands beside
him. Margot has her arm around Richie's shoulder. She smokes a
cigarette. Raleigh stands next to Dudley. Eli stands next to Walter.
The priest is on crutches.*

*Chas looks to Ari and Uzi standing a few yards away. He nods.
Ari and Uzi fire several shots into the air with Chas' and Royal's old
B.B. guns.*

*Royal's gravestone sits in a wheelbarrow next to a pile of dirt. It reads
Royal O'Reilly Tenenbaum (1932–2001). Epitaph: Died tragically
rescuing his family from the wreckage of a destroyed sinking battleship.
The priest sees this and hesitates. He looks puzzled. He smiles slightly.*

*Richie throws a white flower into the grave. They all stand in silence
for a minute before they turn away and walk to their waiting cars.*